PRAISE FOR *I AM FOUND*

I Am Found is a uniquely powerful study for women of all ages who long to fully experience freedom from shame and confidence in Christ. The format includes rich references to Scripture, poignant illustrations, and thought-provoking questions for personal and small group reflection. Women who fully engage in this study will have transformed thinking that results in mature Christian living. I highly recommend this resource!

CAROL KENT
Speaker and author of *Becoming a Woman of Influence*

Whether the idea of being found fills your heart with joy or gives you a sense of dread, this book is for you. Tackling shame head on from the beginning, Laura shows you why being found is so good, especially if you hold the notion that if God found *out* who you really are, He'd hightail it the other direction. Over and over again, the message that God is for you and not against you reverberates through the soul as you read, take apart, and truly digest God's Word. This is a study that helps you silence the clamor and lies that fill your mind so that you can clearly see God's love for you and desire to be found each and every day.

JEN FERGUSON
Coauthor of *Pure Eyes, Clean Heart: A Couple's Journey to Freedom from Pornography*

Laura Dingman has put into our hands a study that takes us on a life-transforming journey that is both biblically accurate and intensely personal. Though presented as a six-week study, *I Am Found* is so much more. Whether doing the study individually or in community with other Christians, *I Am Found* has the potential of impacting the reader's life in ways never before experienced. Having known and worked with Laura for more than twenty years, I celebrate the day when "she was found" and began serving Jesus Christ in vocational ministry.

GARY L. JOHNSON
Senior Minister, Indian Creek Christian Church, Indianapolis, IN

Ever since the days of Adam and Eve, humans have displayed a dogged propensity to hide ourselves from God and from each other. We often do this out of a deep sense of shame that comes from below, not above. If you're tired of hiding and ready to experience a more authentic and vulnerable life, then you can't afford not to experience Laura Dingman's *I Am Found*. It will lovingly lead you to embrace the life God intends for you to live. Get ready to step out of the shadows!

JONATHAN MERRITT
Author of *Jesus Is Better than You Imagined* and contributing writer for The Atlantic

The lies of the enemy swirl in our head. "You'll never be enough." "You're not smart." "You're ugly." "You're too far gone." In *I Am Found*, Laura Dingman confidently walks you through Scripture to debunk each falsehood, restoring your heart and soul to a place of rest. Perfect for your small group or women's study, this book allows you to gather your girlfriends to dive into Truth together. You'll discover how deeply you're loved, leaving the lies of the past behind. What a joy to be really found by God, knowing His plans are good!

CHERIE LOWE
Author of *Slaying the Debt Dragon*

In an age of selfies, personal promotion, and excessive approval-seeking, it is harder than ever to ground our identity in the right place. This study offers us rich wisdom rooted in Laura's personal journey and in the words of Scripture. I deeply respect the work Laura has done, and continues to do, to honestly face her own shame and the destructive voices in her head—replacing them with the truth that she is a valuable child of God. Dig into this study with great anticipation for what God will do in your heart!

NANCY BEACH
Leadership Coach and author of *Gifted to Lead* and *An Hour on Sunday*

The passion Laura feels for women to be free and whole in Christ is infectious. God has given her a call to minister to women who have been told they are not enough, not worthy of true freedom, and too much so they must hide parts of themselves from our Creator and others. Laura lets God use her in powerful ways to dispel those lies and introduce us to a Jesus who wants us to enjoy being truly known by Him and those around us. This Spirit-filled study and Laura's wise words will resonate with you, change you, and free you to experience life in a new, profound way. It has been a blessing to me, and I know it will be for others as well.

MARY GRAHAM
Blogger at trustychucks.com and writer for the *Huffington Post*

Laura Dingman's story of being found by the God who knows, who loves, and who redeems all our stories has found its way into the creation of this excellent study, *I Am Found*. She invited others to join her and now invites you into this process of coming out of hiding, and the journey of being found by Him. The integration of God's Word, personal practice, and community open space for transformation in Him so that you can more fully live the life God intended for you.

SIBYL TOWNER
Coauthor of *Listen To My Life* and codirector of The Springs Retreat Center, Oldenburg, IN

i am found

QUITTING THE GAME OF HIDE AND SEEK

WITH GOD AND OTHERS

LAURA DINGMAN

MOODY PUBLISHERS

CHICAGO

Edited by Pam Pugh
Cover design: Dean Renninger and Erik M. Peterson
Interior design: Erik M. Peterson
Author photo: Kaitlyn Huff
Cover photo of watercolor leaves copyright © 2014 by Alita Ong / Stocksy (348070). All rights reserved.

Library of Congress Cataloging-in-Publication Data

Names: Dingman, Laura, author.
Title: I am found : quitting the game of hide and seek with God and others / Laura Dingman.
Description: Chicago : Moody Publishers, 2016.
Identifiers: LCCN 2016006855 (print) | LCCN 2016012880 (ebook) | ISBN 9780802414687 | ISBN 9780802494665-0
Subjects: LCSH: Shame--Religious aspects--Christianity--Textbooks. | Shame in the Bible--Textbooks.
Classification: LCC BT714 .D56 2016 (print) | LCC BT714 (ebook) | DDC 248.4--dc23
LC record available at http://lccn.loc.gov/2016006855

We hope you enjoy this book from Moody Publishers. Our goal is to provide high-quality, thought-provoking books and products that connect truth to your real needs and challenges. For more information on other books and products written and produced from a biblical perspective, go to www.moodypublishers.com or write to:

Moody Publishers
820 N. LaSalle Boulevard
Chicago, IL 60610

1 3 5 7 9 10 8 6 4 2

Printed in the United States of America

For the Tribe Crazy Train:
Thank you for locked shields in difficult seasons
& for making it safe to come out of hiding.
I love you all.

CONTENTS

TO YOU, THE ONE WHO LONGS TO BE FOUND

When my daughter, Abigail, was about a year old, I started playing peekaboo with her. I would hide her face under a blanket and say, "Where is Abigail?" After a few seconds of building anticipation, I would pull the blanket down for the big reveal and say, "There she is!" She would just bellow with giggles—one of my favorite sounds in the world.

As she grew, her peekaboo game morphed into hide and seek. She would hide and just wait. Every night before bed, she would hide in her closet or under her bed and wait for us to come in and find her. She would then squeal with delight when we finally did. We always knew where she was, but she hid anyway, believing she had tricked us.

For Abigail, it wasn't about hiding. If it was, she probably would have been more creative about where she hid. For her, it was about being found. She hid so we would come after her and *find her*.

Every kid plays hide and seek. It's a rite of passage. Although the aim of the game is *not* to be found, how fun would it be to play a game of hide and seek where you spent days hiding without ever being discovered? I'm certain it would be the loneliest game ever.

As Abigail has grown, something has changed. She doesn't hide as much for fun anymore—she hides when she gets in trouble. It's her first response when faced with the reality of her sin. She's already been introduced to shame. It's not like we sat down with her and explained what shame is. She is wired to understand it. When she has done something wrong, we can't find her. Typically, she is hiding in the same places she hid when she longed to be found—in her closet or under the bed—but now she makes it clear she'd rather stay hidden. Strangely, I think she still aches to be found, even though she tells us otherwise. She wants to know we're

coming after her, that we still love her. She longs to trade her shame for grace.
I respond the same way. In the moments I feel the weight of humiliation for the
wrongs I have done, I want to crawl in a hole, hoping no one can see me. I hide.
I pray no one notices. I work harder to make sure you can't see it.

Sometimes, it just feels easier to stay in the dark so no one will know our business.

Maybe, like me, you play this game of hide and seek. Perhaps you're just as
familiar with it as I am. If you are, you're probably less than thrilled I've just
described the very thing you hope no one knows you do.

Can I be honest? I'm less than thrilled. Right now I would rather crawl under
a rock than talk about being found. The truth is, this topic—how and why we
hide—is a difficult one. It digs at the places in our hearts we just don't want people
seeing. We don't want to unearth what we've buried. We would rather just leave it
alone. Leave it unseen.

But underneath the gunky exterior lies a beautiful nugget of truth.
We really are longing to be found.

Not found out, not exposed, but *found*.

Found and seen.

    Found and accepted.

      Found and understood.

        Found and championed.

          Found and deeply loved.

What if I told you being found this way is possible? These pages will explore how we got here and why we hide. We'll discover who's involved in this game we play and what their roles are. We'll discuss what it looks like to live as though we've been found. We'll consider how we can cultivate a community around us that encourages us to come out of hiding.

Each week will explore truths to shape our understanding of what the Bible says about real spiritual community and how to live in it. These steps will mold your understanding at a greater level. Walking through those pages with the Holy Spirit will allow you to hear from Him where you need to grow and change. He will add color to the picture where my words are lacking. He knows you and loves you deeply. He will walk with you through this excursion.

Life moves at a rapid rate these days. You will be encouraged to take time to listen and linger with God in the pages of Scripture throughout the study as we learn to live differently.

I am praying for you, dear reader, as you embark on this journey. My deep hope for you is that you will come out of hiding and start living the gloriously free life God intended for you to live. I trust God will show you how to strip away shame as you trade it for grace through these pages.

We don't have to hide anymore. Jesus is waiting to show us how to live this kind of life where we are free. And we are aching for it. Let's take hands and walk together out of this foreboding tunnel of hiding. It's a little dark in here. I know the light will seem bright to our squinting eyes as we emerge, but I believe the healing warmth the light brings will restore us. In the end, it *will* be worth it. Freedom is always worth it.

Laura

USING THIS BOOK

I'm so glad you've decided to go through this study! Over the next six weeks, I invite you to dig in each day. If you miss a session, don't be discouraged, and don't give up! Just come back the next day and pick up where you left off. For each week we'll have an introduction to set up Day 1 and the rest of the week, which consists of five daily sessions to help you unpack the theme for the week while giving you a foundation of biblical truth on which to build.

We'll also memorize a verse or two each week. Take a moment every day to review the verse for the week. We want the truths we are memorizing to seep into our souls.

At the end of each week's lessons, we will encounter "Truth, Lies, and Action." This section is a look at the truths learned for the week, at a primary lie we need to exchange for the truth, and an opportunity for an action step to bring each of us a little closer to living as though we are found. This section can be done separately or as a part of your study on Day 5. The important thing is that you take a moment to reflect on what God has shown you and how He invites you to move forward. Taking the time to recognize the truths you've learned, the lies you're letting go of, and the action steps that will solidify it all holds great importance for your journey.

There will be some days you will need your Bible and other times when the reading is printed for you. You might want a journal to document your journey as you go. There is no substitute for spending time at the feet of Jesus to see what He has to say about these things, and in doing so, you will reap a greater harvest. I trust the Holy Spirit to speak in ways my words cannot. Ask Him to help you come out of hiding as you engage in this journey.

fig leaves

don't hide anything

"Those who look to him are radiant; their faces are never covered with shame." **PSALM 34:5**

Shame is universal. Everyone experiences it. While the causes may vary, the results are the same. I'm looking forward to journeying in this first week of the study together, when we will be going all the way back to the beginning of shame in Eden. Where did this all begin and why? Why are we still hiding? How have we tried to cover our own shame? What does God say about it all? Who else is involved?

I'm grateful for your courage to journey with me in these pages. My prayer for you this week is that you will begin to believe, as you look to our loving Savior, your face is radiant and never covered with shame.

INTRODUCTION TO WEEK 1

WHY DO WE HIDE?

There you are. It's middle school all over again. You're standing in the center of a crowded cafeteria. Boys and girls point fingers as they double over laughing. You can hear the sound of their laughter. Your face grows hot. You feel a slight breeze. A little colder than usual. You wonder what's going on, how you got here. What is happening? Then you look down and discover you have neglected to put on a stitch of clothing. You stand stark naked, uncovered. You're also the unfortunate centerpiece of a jam-packed middle school lunch period.

We've all had our own version of this dream at some point in time. It varies in scenario, but is rooted in similarity. The possibility of being exposed petrifies us. Our fear connects to physical exposure but reaches into other areas as well. We just don't like to be laid bare. It shames us.

It hasn't always been this way. Imagining life without this embarrassing fear seems difficult. Life without shame existed in the beginning, though it's impossible for us to understand.

Let's set the stage: In the opening act of creation, God crafts beauty everywhere. A garden is planted with trees, plants, and flowers watered by rivers, lakes, and streams. Living creatures frolic, and everything is in perfect harmony, and God proclaims His creation to be good. God breathes life into Adam's nostrils and man enters the scene. God proclaims it all to be very good. Not just *good*, as it has been every other time, but *very* good (Genesis 1:31).

The Creator understands the man needs a helper (Genesis 2:18). One by one, the other living creatures parade before Adam. As he names them all, each is assessed as a potential partner for him. After all are considered, no suitable helper is discovered (Genesis 2:20). So out of Adam's own flesh and bone, God designs a woman to be a perfect complement for him.

In the midst of the creation account sits a tiny verse, seemingly unimportant at first: "Adam and his wife were both naked, and *they felt no shame*" (Genesis 2:25). Unclothed, uncovered, man and woman walk around feeling absolutely no shame whatsoever. Granted, no one points and laughs at them, but still, disgrace and humiliation are not a part of the equation at this point. No shame. No masks. No hiding. No pointing and laughing.

Enter the serpent. His arrival on the scene changes everything. To fully comprehend the shift in the story, we have to understand a little about the serpent's nature. Genesis 3:1 says he was more "crafty" than any of the wild animals the Lord God had made. The word "crafty" in Hebrew is '*aruwm*, meaning subtle, shrewd, and sly. He isn't a crafty DIY-er, but he *is* an artist of sorts. He just happens to be an artful liar. With his appearance, doubt, lies, and shame enter the scene for the first time, disrupting the harmony of Eden.

He engages in a conversation with the unsuspecting woman. He inquires, "Did God *really* say, 'You must not eat from any tree in the garden'?" (Genesis 3:1). At first, the question doesn't phase her. She doesn't miss a beat. She repeats God's instructions. "We may eat fruit from the trees in the garden, but God did say, 'You must not eat fruit from the tree that is in the middle of the garden, and you must not touch it, or you will die'" (Genesis 3:2–3). For whatever reason Eve adds "and you must not touch it," her response proves that she knows and understands full well the guidelines God gave to Adam (Genesis 2:16–17). After all, she's been living by them.

Immediately, the sly serpent makes a simple statement that changes everything: "You will not certainly die." He pronounces a half-truth. That's what makes him an artful liar. There seems to be a tiny nugget of truth in what he speaks. The woman would not die *immediately* after eating the fruit from this tree, but she would die eventually if she ate it. Then the crafty creature whispers to the woman, "God knows that when you eat from it your eyes will be opened, and you will be like God, knowing good and evil" (Genesis 3:5). In other words, God didn't tell you the whole truth. He's holding out on you. He's keeping from you something you could have.

Most likely, before this moment, the woman had never considered the fruit on the tree. It was off-limits, so she never even wondered what would happen if she ate it. God said to stay away, so she did. He set a boundary, and she complied without question. But now, because of the voice of the shrewd serpent, her curiosity awakens. Suddenly, she views the tree differently. "When the woman saw that the fruit of the tree was good for food and pleasing to the eye, and also desirable for gaining wisdom, she took some and ate it" (Genesis 3:6). Before her diabolical dialogue with the serpent, she thought nothing of the fruit. She was content to do as God had said. Now having spoken with the schemer, she suddenly wants what isn't hers to take. Her curiosity stirs her desire. She craves the fruit that would make her to be like God. Fearful of missing out, she wants what the serpent told her God is withholding. In her naivety, she shares her discovery with Adam and hands him a piece of fruit.

For a split second, the succulent fruit tastes delectable, sugary sweet and crisp. But the enjoyment fades instantly when shame overwhelms them. With the knowledge they have gained, they discover they are naked, exposed. Before the fruit, they were naked—they just didn't know they weren't supposed to be. They had no reason to feel ashamed. Now the desire to hide and cover their nakedness overtakes them.

> God continues to demonstrate deep compassion, unrelenting mercy, and unbelievable grace.

In an effort to fix the problem—to conceal it—they create coverings for themselves from fig leaves. Fig leaves are about five to ten inches long and four to seven inches wide. They aren't enormous or all that sturdy. Adam and his wife sew some together anyway, attempting to camouflage themselves.

As they hear God strolling through the garden, the real game of hide and seek begins. At the sound of God's footsteps, fear hits hard and they hide from God among the trees of the garden, hoping God won't notice their new outfits.

God calls to the man and asks, "Where are you?" The all-knowing, omniscient

God already knows where Adam is hiding and what has been broken in Eden, but He questions anyway, giving the man an opportunity to openly admit what's transpired—an opportunity to come clean. It takes some deeper inquiry to get to the root of the problem. Adam starts with the obvious: "I heard you in the garden, and I was afraid because I was naked; so I hid" (Genesis 3:10). Pretty sure the fig leaf getup was a dead giveaway for that one. God digs a little deeper, giving him yet another chance to tell the truth, asking, "Who told you that you were naked? Have you eaten from the tree that I commanded you not to eat from?" The straight answer would have been yes. "Yes, I ate from the tree. I did what You told me not to do." But Adam's shame speaks up. "Well, you know that woman You put here with me? She gave me a piece of fruit from the tree and I ate it." In his humiliation, Adam cannot own his wrongdoing. He shifts the blame to the woman. Following suit, the woman blames the serpent.

The scene is no longer very good. The plot of Eden shifts. Conflict arises. The man, the woman, and the serpent face the consequences of their choices. God lays out a curse for each of them. Suffering accompanies their shame. Hardship clouds the once perfect garden. Hope is distant, and shame is very near.

Then God does something extraordinary. In the midst of this bleak situation, He extends grace after grace. He begins with the woman who made the choice that changed everything. Until this point, she is nameless. She is only referred to as "the woman." God allows restoration as Adam gives her the name Eve. In the midst of her shame, the curse, and the mess, *God allows her to be named,* giving her an identity. Not only does Adam give her an identity, but he gives her a purpose along with her name. He names her Eve because she will be the mother of all the living (Genesis 3:20). God could have left her in her disgrace with the curse as her future, but He didn't. He continues to demonstrate deep compassion, unrelenting mercy, and unbelievable grace. He allows her to be granted a new beginning, a new life.

Then God pours grace over both Eve and Adam by making new garments for them. God grasps the ineffective nature of their fig leaf attire. He recognizes what lies ahead for them both and wearing fig leaves will not be helpful. They require more durable coverings. So the first blood sacrifice to cover sin is made. Full of grace, God fashions garments of animal skins for Adam and Eve, replacing their inadequate fig leaf costumes.

The last act of grace in the garden is surprising. God actually kicks Adam and Eve out of Eden. They are banished. After they are driven out, God places guardians around the tree of life. It seems a little harsh. Can't Adam and Eve just stay in the garden? But God knows what will happen if Adam and Eve eat from the Tree of Life now. This tree was not forbidden before they took the bite from the Tree of Knowledge of Good and Evil. They ate freely from the Tree of Life. They knew its fruit. Eating from both trees proved to be a toxic combination. Because they have experienced shame, living forever isn't a great idea. In His beautiful grace, God protects Adam and Eve from that kind of life. Even though they will now experience death, they will not suffer shame and disgrace for eternity. And God has a plan for eternity.

Shame, guilt, and humiliation didn't stay in Eden. When sin entered, it never exited, plaguing every generation since the first one Eve birthed, including yours and mine. With sin comes shame. They are inseparable. It's a cause-and-effect relationship. I sin, therefore I feel guilt and shame. It's a cycle that's all too familiar.

The motivation of characters in any story matters. Motivation colors the choices of each person in the plot. In the midst of this well-known progression of events, knowing the motivation of the characters in Eden aids our understanding of our own battle with shame. Man and woman wanted to be like God. Before it was so blatantly pointed out, they were fairly oblivious. However, once the serpent spoke it out loud, Eve just couldn't shake the thought. There was something God had that they didn't. Adam didn't speak up, either. They both took the bait because they desired the knowledge of good and evil God had. Was God withholding something good from them? They didn't want to miss what could have been theirs. Once they took the fruit, they realized being like God was impossible, and guilt and disgrace washed over them.

The serpent had one motivation. He was the opposition, the enemy. He was against the woman, against the man, against God. His primary goal was to defeat them all, even if it meant turning them against one another in the process. He was bent on destruction at any cost, relishing the outcome as it all crumbled. Pure evil.

God, on the other hand, was for man and woman. Every choice He made, every word He spoke to Adam and Eve, showed He was for them. He had their best interest in mind. He lovingly lavished grace on them, restoring them and protecting them in the process. At the same time, He declared the serpent the enemy. While cursing him, God proclaimed and prophesied the crafty creature's demise.

Our story is no different. Our motivation matches that of Adam and Eve. We choose what we want because we don't want to miss something. We sin because we want to be like God. When we fail, which is inevitable, we experience shame.

An enemy lurks for us, as well. He opposes God and seeks to destroy our lives because of it. He consistently stirs doubt and speaks deception so the cycle of shame continues.

But God is for us. He showers grace over us, relentless in His loving pursuit of us. His mercy never ceases. Even when it seems as though we are being punished, like the garden banishment, God protects. God provides coverings for our shame.

Psalm 34:5 tells us, "Those who look to him are radiant; their faces are never covered with shame."

Remembering God is for us is challenging when wrestling with shame. Even if you don't fully believe that God is for you yet, hang on to that truth as we continue this journey. The key is to look to Him as we go. Keep your eyes on God, and the enemy's voice will lessen and shame *will* lose its power.

LINGER AND LEARN

How have you hidden from God?

Take a moment to write out Isaiah 43:1. Reflect on the words and circle the ones that stand out. How do you feel knowing God has redeemed you, covering you with grace and has, like Eve, given you a new name?

SHAME'S THE NAME OF THE GAME

Recently, Abigail and I were shopping at Kohl's. We had a cartload of things and, well, I had consumed a great deal of water prior to shopping. Let's just say a grand emergency developed. We proceeded to the restroom. With Abigail in tow, I left the cart in the hallway, flew into the bathroom, and found a stall. Just as I sat down, I heard her little voice calmly ask, "Mommy, what are these funny things on the wall?" Then she paused and said, "Are we in the boy's bathroom?" As the words left her lips, I heard a low voice say, "Why yes, my dear, you are."

Panic flooded as I leapt to my feet and covered myself. With my face the color of tomatoes, I grabbed Abigail's hand, and we darted out the door. After our escape, Abigail firmly requested we leave immediately. "Can we just get out of here, Mommy? Like, right now?" she begged. Then she said it. Words I had never heard out of her tiny mouth: "I'm just so ashamed." Not embarrassed, but ashamed. We made a mistake and got caught. The natural response was to run and hide.

In the Introduction, we discussed Genesis 2:25–3:24. This passage contains the very first game of hide and seek recorded in the Bible. We discovered the man and woman felt no shame prior to this game (Genesis 2:25). There was no reason for it. There was no sin. No brokenness. Man and woman were one with God and had no reason to hide.

Then the serpent brings something new to the party. He enters the scene and begins spinning a web of deceit, and doubt begins to build in Eve's mind. She doesn't quite know what to do with it. She has no precedent for dealing with doubt. She flounders and eventually bites into the lie. She shares the lie with Adam, and together they are introduced to shame.

Shame is an interesting thing. Take a look at the dictionary.com definition of shame:

shame [sheym]: *noun*

1. The painful feeling arising from the consciousness of something dishonorable, improper, ridiculous, etc., done by oneself or another.
2. Susceptibility to this feeling.
3. Disgrace, ignominy.
4. A fact or circumstance bringing disgrace or regret.[1]

Yikes. Even the definition does something in your stomach. Shame likes to stay in secret places. It likes to lurk in the dark and spring up when no one else is around. It waits for well-timed attacks.

Here are some synonyms for shame:

confusion	contempt	guilt	humiliation	blot
remorse	scandal	stigma	abashment	irritation
discredit	dishonor	infamy	reproach	self-disgust

"Shame is the intensely painful feeling or experience of believing that we are flawed and therefore unworthy of love and belonging." [2]

READ GENESIS 2:25–3:8

Something changed in Adam and Eve, and they felt shame after their mistake.

How do you feel shame? How does it usually show up? What circumstances typically surround your shame?

---

1. Shame. Dictionary.com., Unabridged. Random House, Inc. http://dictionary.reference.com/browse/shame.

2. Brené Brown, *Daring Greatly* (New York, NY: Gotham Books, 2012), 69.

When Adam's and Eve's eyes were opened, their first reaction was to cover up what brought them shame. At first, they covered their nakedness. Then they heard God and they hid.

How do you hide?

From whom do you hide? From God? From others?

What circumstances cause you to hide most?

Take a look at the memory verse for this week:

Those who look to him are radiant; their faces are never covered with shame. (Psalm 34:5)

How does this truth change the way you view shame?

Take a few moments to ask God to reveal how you have allowed shame to keep you from His best for you. Ask Him to show you how to begin walking with your eyes on Him and not on your shame.

Lord Jesus, You have told me I do not have to live in shame. Although it follows me around pretty much daily, You have made a way for me to cast my shame on You. You paid a great price so I could live blamelessly and walk without shame. Thank You for releasing me from that burden. Help me not to wear garments of shame any longer. I want You to clothe me with Your righteousness. Amen.

WEEK 1 | DAY 2

CLOTHES OF GRACE

Yesterday we learned about shame. We learned definitions of shame and got real about how we feel shame and hide because of it. Today we continue digging into the first game of hide and seek.

Read Genesis 3:7–10 as paraphrased in The Message:

> Immediately the two of them did "see what's really going on"—saw themselves naked! They sewed fig leaves together as makeshift clothes for themselves. When they heard the sound of God strolling in the garden in the evening breeze, the Man and his Wife hid in the trees of the garden, hid from God. God called to the Man: "Where are you?" He said, "I heard you in the garden and I was afraid because I was naked. And I hid."

Read the text again and highlight or circle the words that pop off the page.

What words or phrases stand out? What do they show you? Why do they stand out?

Notice Adam and Eve's reaction to hearing God: they hid. First, they tried to clothe themselves in a feeble attempt to cover their nakedness. Then when they heard God, they hid. Prior to the entrance of sin and shame, Adam and Eve welcomed God's presence in the garden. Perhaps they even *delighted* in it. But things are different now. Their shame induces fear and a frantic response.

Knowing God is omniscient, it's strange God would ask Adam where he was. God has infinite knowledge, so He obviously knew where Adam was hiding. But in His grace and mercy, He gave Adam a chance to come clean. God allowed Adam the opportunity to confess his shame.

God does the same with Eve. When Adam tells God of her role in the fiasco, God turns to her and asks, "What is this you have done?" Eve confesses she ate from the tree.

The next part of the text (Genesis 3:14–19) lays out a bit of their future. They will carry consequences with them as a result of their choices. All three of them: the serpent, the woman, and the man. They each had a distinct role in the event and, as a result, they have distinct consequences.

And then something interesting happens:

> The Lord God made garments of skin for Adam and his wife and clothed them. And the Lord God said, "The man has now become like one of us, knowing good and evil. He must not be allowed to reach out his hand and take also from the tree of life and eat, and live forever." So the Lord God banished him from the Garden of Eden to work the ground from which he had been taken. After he drove the man out, he placed on the east side of the Garden of Eden cherubim and a flaming sword flashing back and forth to guard the way to the tree of life. (Genesis 3:21–24)

In the midst of this curse—this reminder of shame—God's great love and mercy arise. He has seen the "makeshift" fig-leaf garments Adam and Eve are sporting, and He knows they just aren't going to cut it for what's ahead.

When I've read Genesis 3:22–24 in the past, I thought God was punishing Adam and Eve for their wrong choices by banishing them from the garden. I think there was something more happening.

> And the Lord God said, "The man has now become like one of us, knowing good and evil. He must not be allowed to reach out his hand and take also from the tree of life and eat, and live forever." (Genesis 3:22)

God was extending breathtaking grace. Bountiful kindness. Beautiful mercy. He knew Adam and Eve were going to be living with the consequences of sin. If they were to take from the tree of life, there would be no end to their suffering. They would not be able to withstand the shame to come.

As a result, God banned them from the garden and placed a safety net around the tree, guaranteeing they would not endure a double dose of distress. He set a new boundary to protect them. But before they were exiled—which was for their own good—He created lasting clothing for them. He helped them cover their shame. He said nothing to them about how ridiculous the fig leaf attempt really was. He simply—in one verse—made garments of skin to clothe them and rid them of their shame.

The first sin. The first game of hide and seek. The first death to cover shame. The first act of great love, redemption, and grace.

How have you hidden from God when you have known He knows anyway?

How has God gently corrected you and protected you like Adam and Eve from your own shameful choices?

PRAYER FOR THE DAY

Lord Jesus, I am beyond grateful for the amazing ways You have continually corrected me with grace and mercy. You have shown Your very great love to me. Thank You that Your love is long and high and wide and deep. May I learn more and more what it really looks like as I grow in the knowledge of Your grace. Cover me so I will not be covered in shame. Clothe me with Your righteousness. Amen.

WEEK 1 | DAY 3

COMING CLEAN

Honesty ranks high on my list of standards. I like people to tell me the truth, even when it's hard. But for someone who values honesty and genuine authenticity so much, I have a hard time telling the truth about myself. Coming clean stinks sometimes. Admitting I have sinned or wronged someone—even in the presence of people I know love me—brings anxiety.

One of the best choices Adam and Eve made after their debacle was coming clean before God. When He inquired what they had done, they faced a choice to tell God the truth or not. While blame shifted, they eventually spoke the truth. They knew God had their best interests in mind, so being straightforward about what had transpired didn't take much convincing.

One of my favorite stories of someone coming clean involves David. David took the long way around, but he eventually got there. Over the next two days we're going to look at David's big shaming moment, how he responded, and what it means for us.

Read 2 Samuel 11:1–27.

How did David try to hide from God and others? What different things did he do to hide?

Did this rid him of his shame? Why?

Read 2 Samuel 12:1–19.

How was David forced to come clean?

How might things have been different for David if he had come clean on his own?

How do you think it affected his relationship with God and others?

How have you acted like David in the past?

What do you need to bring to God as you come clean before Him in this present moment?

Merciful Jesus, I know You see the dark places in my soul. I want to believe You love me anyway, but that's difficult for me. Teach me to trust You. Show me how to tell You the truth about what I've done outside of Your will for my life. Help me to know I am covered by grace. Help me to come clean. Amen.

CONFESSION CAN BE BEAUTIFUL

Today, we continue our study of David's response to shame. When we left David yesterday, he had lost his son as a result of his own sinful actions. He had fasted and prayed and pleaded with God to spare his son, but God did not. We pick up in 2 Samuel 12:20:

> Then David got up from the ground. After he had washed, put on lotions and changed his clothes, he went into the house of the Lord and worshiped. Then he went to his own house, and at his request they served him food, and he ate.

Around the time of this incident, David penned Psalm 51, one of the most beautiful confessional prayers in the Bible. David recognized his intense need for God to do the miraculous and take away his shame.

Today we'll walk through David's confessional prayer in Psalm 51 and pray through it ourselves. Our struggle with sin and shame is no different from David's. Maybe you feel as though your sin is greater than David's. *It isn't.* Maybe you feel as though it's not as great as David's. *It is.* Sin is separation from God, and there are not degrees of separation. Separation is separation. God views it the same. No matter what your sin is or my sin is, God sees it as sin. It all requires the same sacrifice from Jesus to make it right.

We want to close the existing gap between our sinful selves and our Holy Creator. Christ has built a bridge for us, and we are forgiven if we are found in Him. This moment, however, is about coming clean before Him. "If we confess our sins, he is faithful and just and will forgive us our sins and purify us from all unrighteousness" (1 John 1:9).[3]

---

3. Perhaps you have not yet surrendered your life to Christ. Romans 8:1 tells us, "There is now no condemnation for those who are in Christ Jesus our Lord." In order to receive the covering for shame we need, we must confess Jesus as Lord and believe He is the Son of God. And then it is important for us to also be obedient to Him in baptism. If you are not yet a follower of Christ and need to make that decision, please take time to talk to someone about this very important decision. Christ is the bridge, but you must accept Him before you can walk across. He is waiting for you—waiting to show grace, mercy, and love.

Find a quiet place to read through Psalm 51 and answer the questions. Be honest. Be brave. Say the things that need to be said. God already knows anyway.

Have mercy on me, O God,
　according to your unfailing love;
according to your great compassion
　blot out my transgressions.
Wash away all my iniquity
　and cleanse me from my sin.
For I know my transgressions,
　and my sin is always before me.

Against you, you only, have I sinned
　and done what is evil in your sight;
so you are right in your verdict
　and justified when you judge.

Surely I was sinful at birth,
　sinful from the time my mother conceived me.

Yet you desired faithfulness even in the womb;
　you taught me wisdom in that secret place.
　—verses 1–6

God, I have rebelled by . . .

I have sinned by . . .

Wash me and cleanse me from . . .

Wash me so I will be whiter than snow. Wash away . . .

Create in me a clean, pure heart, O God. Rid my heart of . . .

Cleanse me with hyssop, and I will be clean;
  wash me, and I will be whiter than snow.
Let me hear joy and gladness;
  let the bones you have crushed rejoice.
Hide your face from my sins
  and blot out all my iniquity.

Create in me a pure heart, O God,
  and renew a steadfast spirit within me.

Do not cast me from your presence
  or take your Holy Spirit from me.
—verses 7–11

Restore to me the joy of your salvation
  and grant me a willing spirit, to sustain me.

Then I will teach transgressors your ways,
  so that sinners will turn back to you.
Deliver me from the guilt of bloodshed, O God,
  you who are God my Savior,
  and my tongue will sing of your righteousness.
Open my lips, Lord,
  and my mouth will declare your praise.
—verses 12–15

I praise You, Jesus. I adore You because . . .

You are . . .

> My sacrifice, O God, is a broken spirit;
>   a broken and contrite heart
>   you, God, will not despise.
>
> May it please you to prosper Zion,
>   to build up the walls of Jerusalem.
> Then you will delight in the sacrifices of the righteous,
>   in burnt offerings offered whole;
>   then bulls will be offered on your altar.
> —verses 16–19

Help me to bring you a broken spirit, a contrite heart. Break my spirit in the areas of . . .

Lord Jesus, thank You. Thank You for making me clean through Your blood sacrifice. You have reached beyond my boundaries and have expanded my idea of grace. Forgive me for the wrongs I have allowed to fester in my spirit. Restore to me the joy of loving You, following You, and living Your story. You are amazing, God. Amen.

WEEK 1 | DAY 5

NO MORE SHAME

One of the ways we learn God is for us is by engaging in His Word. Throughout this study, we will be engaging Scripture in a variety of ways. Taking the time to sit in the presence of God and His Word will produce transformative results in each of us. There is no substitute for listening to what the Holy Spirit has to say to us through the power of Scripture.

One way we will encounter Scripture will be through a four-part process. We will listen, linger, learn, and then live. Let's dig in.

Read through the given passage four times. Four different sets of questions will help you encounter the text in a fresh, new way and bring life to your bones. It's not about simply completing the repetition. It's about lingering and listening to see what needs to be learned and ultimately lived. We want to be changed by our time in God's Word.

Today's text is Psalm 34. Psalm 34:5 is our memory verse, so let's take a moment to discover its context.

LISTEN

Read Psalm 34. Sit quietly for a moment before you begin. Ask the Holy Spirit to speak and show you what the Lord wants for you in this passage. Mark words or phrases that stand out as you read.

I will extol the Lord at all times;
  his praise will always be on
my lips.

I will glory in the Lord;
  let the afflicted hear and rejoice.

Glorify the Lord with me;
  let us exalt his name together.
I sought the Lord, and he
  answered me;
  he delivered me from all
my fears.

Those who look to him are radiant;
  their faces are never covered with shame.

This poor man called, and the Lord heard him;
  he saved him out of all his troubles.
The angel of the Lord encamps around those who fear him,
  and he delivers them.
Taste and see that the Lord is good;
  blessed is the one who takes refuge in him.
Fear the Lord, you his holy people,
  for those who fear him lack nothing.
The lions may grow weak and hungry,
  but those who seek the Lord lack no good thing.

Come, my children, listen to me;
  I will teach you the fear of the Lord.
Whoever of you loves life
  and desires to see many good days,

keep your tongue from evil
  and your lips from telling lies.

Turn from evil and do good;
  seek peace and pursue it.
The eyes of the Lord are on the righteous,
  and his ears are attentive to their cry;
but the face of the Lord is against those who do evil,
  to blot out their name from the earth.

The righteous cry out, and the Lord hears them;
  he delivers them from all their troubles.
The Lord is close to the brokenhearted
  and saves those who are crushed in spirit.
The righteous person may have many troubles,
  but the Lord delivers him from them all;

he protects all his bones,
  not one of them will be broken.

Evil will slay the wicked;
  the foes of the righteous will be condemned.
The Lord will rescue his servants;
  no one who takes refuge in him will be condemned.

LINGER

Read the passage again out loud. Are the same words or phrases you marked the first time still standing out? Write them down. How do these words or phrases apply to your life right now?

LEARN

As you read the text for a third time, ask yourself, "How is God inviting me to respond? What does He want me to be learning from this?" Write out what comes to mind.

LIVE

Read the passage one last time and answer these questions:

Why is God showing me this now?

What does this mean for my life?

What needs to change in my life?

How do I need to live differently?

Lord Jesus, I'm crying out to You. I know You hear me even when it doesn't seem like You do. Be close. Don't crush my spirit. Deliver me and protect me when I am unable to protect myself. I want to taste and see that You are good. You deliver me from all my fears. Amen.

TRUTH, LIES, AND ACTION

Shame is ingrained in our thinking. We have carried it our entire lives. In order to begin thinking differently, we must spend some time redirecting our thoughts. This new thinking requires that we replace the lies with truth and take action.

At the end of each week, we are going to look at three very specific things:

TRUTH: A new way of looking at a truth from God's Word to replace the →
LIES: We want to name the lies we've believed and reclaim them with new truths to move us into→
ACTION: Because faith without works is dead (James 2:20), we want to be people of action. We will be looking today and tomorrow at specific action steps we can take to come out of hiding.

TRUTH: Our memory verse says, *"Those who look to him are radiant; their faces are never covered with shame" (Psalm 34:5).* TRUTH tells us if we are looking to Jesus, our faces are *never* covered with shame.

What truths did you discover this week?

LIES: The LIE tells us we will be covered with shame forever and we will carry it for the rest of our lives.

What lies did you discover this week?

ACTION: Over the next few days, consider one or more of these action steps to help you name your shame and come out of hiding:

- Find one trustworthy friend and share something you learned about yourself this week.
- Do you need to tell someone something, but you've been putting it off because of shame? Find the person and share what you've been withholding.
- Do you need to be honest with God about something? Are you trying to hide something from Him? Take some time today to share it with Him. Tell Him the truth and ask Him to cover and clothe you with His grace and mercy, just like He did with Adam and Eve.
- Do you need to set in place a new boundary (like God set for Adam and Eve in the garden) so you will not continue to sin? Of course, we cannot be perfect, but borders and accountability help limit our options sometimes. Ask God what your boundary should be. Commit to Him that boundary and share it with another person so you can be held accountable.

Write about your ACTION step below. Share why you chose it and what the results were.

PRAYER FOR THE DAY

Lord Jesus, You taught me so much this week. I want to come clean before You. I want to taste and see that You are good. I want to feel You covering me with Your grace—clothing me with Your love. Thank You for never giving up on me, even when I fail a thousand times. Amen.

know

your enemy

"But now, this is what the Lord says—he who created you, Jacob, he who formed you, Israel: 'Do not fear, for I have redeemed you; I have summoned you by name; you are mine.'" **Isaiah 43:1**

"Be alert and of sober mind. Your enemy the devil prowls around like a roaring lion looking for someone to devour." **1 Peter 5:8**

Welcome to the second week of our study. This week can change the game. You'll discover many things, both old and new. My deep prayer for you is anything old will be made new and the new things will feel like you've been wearing them around forever, like your favorite sweatshirt.

Some of what we are going to encounter this week may seem basic, but understanding it in a new light is what moves us forward. I hope this week you will allow God to find you—and allow you to stop running from Him. I'm also praying for you to see how subtle and sly the enemy is. His tactics go unnoticed so much of the time, and we chalk it up to life circumstances or negative thinking. He wants to destroy what God is doing in you. The good news is it's not his to destroy. Our God is bigger and stronger and mightier and has unlimited resources. Take the time to truly sit at the feet of Jesus and allow His truth to wash over you. May your megaphone remain firmly in your hand this week as you declare the praises of our glorious Savior and tell His story to the world.

INTRODUCTION TO WEEK 2

HOW CAN WE WIN THE WAR ON SHAME?

A lump outlining the familiar shape of a four-year-old girl sat under the blanket trying to be still. Her tiny toes poked around the edge. "You can't see me, Momma," her little voice squealed. I could see her plainly. I could see her squirming, trying to stay covered, but Abigail believed with her whole heart that I couldn't see her. Because she couldn't see me, she assumed I couldn't see her.

At times, we have the same mentality with God. Since we cannot see Him directly, we believe He can't see us. We think we can somehow hide from Him. In Psalm 139, David shares his inability to keep anything from God. God sees all of him. God knows everything about David, from where he walks to what he thinks to what crosses his lips even before it does so. Then David questions, "Where can I go from Your Spirit? Where can I flee from your presence?" (verse 7) He realizes he can't go anywhere on earth or in heaven where God will not be with him, knowing him, seeing him. Regardless of the place or the depth of darkness in it, God will be present and will shine His light.

The same rings true for you. Nothing in all of creation is hidden from God's sight (Hebrews 4:13). You cannot escape God. You can't outrun Him, because He never relents. You can't choose anything so out of bounds He will not follow you there, because He fiercely pursues you. Remember, God is for you. He is good and has good things in mind for you. Even when trouble comes your way or worse yet, you choose it, *He works it for your good* (Romans 8:28). We saw this truth demonstrated before in God's response to Adam and Eve. Every move He made was for their benefit. He does the same for you.

> **God is for us. God will restore us in the midst of our guilt and shame, making us strong, firm, and steadfast because He is for us.**

Like the garments of skin God made, God fashioned a covering for our shame in Jesus Christ. Because He was blameless, He could give His innocent life to cover our shame, and now we can approach God with confidence, and we don't have to hide anymore (Hebrews 4:14–16). We have a High Priest who grasps our weaknesses. Jesus wore the same skin we do. He walked the temptation-laden path we walk. He understands. He sees. He knows. He intercedes. This is clear evidence of someone who is for you.

Like God, our enemy the devil cannot be seen directly, so we think he can't see us either. Or worse yet, we forget he's there entirely and lack any awareness of his schemes because of our limited vision. Unlike God, the enemy opposes us. Forgetting he is on the scene can be dangerous. He is on the prowl like a lion searching for prey to devour (1 Peter 5:8). His tempting bait brings shame and disgrace. We fall short, and he's right there to remind us. When he does, Peter instructs us to resist and stand firm. He reminds us we can stand firm knowing others stand with us. We are not alone in this fight (1 Peter 5:9). God is for us, Peter proclaims. God will restore us in the midst of our guilt and shame, making us strong, firm, and steadfast because He is for us (1 Peter 5:10).

Knowing our enemy shines light into the dark places where he lurks. Understanding how our enemy operates better equips us to stand firm in the face of his scheming. The devil is our opponent, our archenemy, an adversary, a foe. He is a destroyer, an accuser, and a slanderer. He fosters harmful designs against us. He engages in hostility, opposing our good. Nothing he sends our way will ever benefit us.

Whether we want to acknowledge it or not, we are in a war. Paul tells us we are not fighting "against flesh and blood, but against the rulers, against the authorities, against the powers of this dark world and against the spiritual forces of evil in the heavenly realms" (Ephesians 6:12).

I don't know much about war. What I do know I've gleaned from books, movies, and the news. My experience is far from firsthand, making it extremely limited and also highly inaccurate, I presume. But even in my incomplete understanding of war, I do know one thing. I know if I am engaged in a war without weapons, I'm toast. Satan's most powerful weapon is the voice of shame. His language is lies. It's his native tongue. He's crafty, remember? The subtle, sly serpent. If he's got a weapon, we need to be armed in the fight as well.

So let's get to know our weaponry.

We find our list of armor in Ephesians 6:10–18.

> Finally, be strong in the Lord and in his mighty power. Put on the full armor of God, so that you can take your stand against the devil's schemes. For our struggle is not against flesh and blood, but against the rulers, against the authorities, against the powers of this dark world and against the spiritual forces of evil in the heavenly realms. Therefore put on the full armor of God, so that when the day of evil comes, you may be able to stand your ground, and after you have done everything, to stand. Stand firm then, with the belt of truth buckled around your waist, with the breastplate of righteousness in place, and with your feet fitted with the readiness that comes from the gospel of peace. In addition to all this, take up the shield of faith, with which you can extinguish all the flaming arrows of the evil one. Take the helmet of salvation and the sword of the Spirit, which is the word of God. And pray in the Spirit on all occasions with all kinds of prayers and requests. With this in mind, be alert and always keep on praying for all the Lord's people.

Paul gives us a practical list of powerful munitions so we will be equipped for the battle we face. Paul's first charge for us is to "be strong in the Lord and in his mighty power" (Ephesians 6:10). God is the source of the victory, not us. He is the Keeper of this arsenal and the power behind it all. Paul reminds us "our struggle is not against flesh and blood, but against the rulers, against the authorities, against the powers of this dark world and against the spiritual forces of evil in the heavenly realms" (verse 12). In order to have a chance of winning in the midst of those against us, we must put on the *full* armor of God. While each of the items Paul lists holds power on its own, they are much more effective when used together.

With this as our foundation, let's take a look at each individual piece.

BELT OF TRUTH

Paul starts with the belt of truth (Ephesians 6:14). Since the devil's language is lies, truth is our best weapon. When he slings the mud, the truth protects. It grounds us. God's Word filters truth for us. When the enemy speaks lies, we fight back with what God says is true. We put on this belt of truth by knowing God's Word and by listening to the Holy Spirit. With it we can sift through the enemy's lies and fight back with truth.

BREASTPLATE OF RIGHTEOUSNESS

The breastplate of righteousness covers our hearts (Ephesians 6:14). If we have put our trust in Christ, we have been made right with God, so we should carry no guilt. Our hearts have been made clean by the work of Christ on the cross. There is no condemnation anymore (Romans 8:1). This breastplate shelters us from shame. Our righteousness comes from God and not from our own merit. He is the Source, the reason we can be covered, and nothing can separate us from His love (Romans 8:39).

SANDALS OF PEACE

Our feet are to be fitted with the readiness, which comes from the gospel of peace (Ephesians 6:15). We are not to be weighed down or anchored by anxiety. God's peace makes us lighter, ready to move at a moment's notice. Our God is greater than anything in this world (1 John 4:4). Isaiah 9:6 reminds us that Christ Himself is the Prince of Peace. And the great passage of Philippians 4:6–7 assures us of His peace beyond all understanding.

SHIELD OF FAITH

The next piece of armor fascinates me. It's the only piece of armor on the list with a description of what we can do with it. We are told the shield of faith "extinguishes all the flaming arrows of the evil one" (Ephesians 6:16). The shield Paul had in mind was a large shield Roman soldiers would use to protect their whole bodies. These shields were four feet tall and two and a half feet wide. They were made of leather-covered wood, reinforced with metal at the top and bottom. The soldiers would soak the shields in water, and the shields effectively stopped burning arrows in combat.[4]

Faith—this assurance of what we hope for and belief in what we cannot see (Hebrews 11:1)—acts like a Roman infantry shield. Faith halts flaming arrows. Faith defends against the weapons meant to destroy us. Faith protects us.

Another amazing fact about Roman shields is their interlocking mechanisms. When soldiers entered combat, each shield would overlap on either side for more effective protection. When locked together, these shields were no longer just defensive—a line of soldiers with interlocked shields could push their way through enemy lines.[5]

An individual soldier with a shield was not as protected as a group of soldiers, and a single soldier had no chance of advancing against the enemy. When soldiers locked shields with other soldiers, however, they were mightier. Their chances of winning the battle increased. The same is true for us. We are not fighting alone, and strength comes from joining together. Others are fighting this battle alongside us. When we recognize who fights with us, we can lock shields with them and we all have a better chance of making it through the battle.

Our faith isn't the only shield either. Psalm 91:4 says, "He will cover you with his feathers, and under his wings you will find refuge; his faithfulness will be your shield and rampart." The faithfulness of God shields us. He is our great protector, shielding us from the battle.

HELMET OF SALVATION

The helmet of salvation protects our minds—the place where our thoughts reside. Our salvation reminds us to whom we belong. When we choose Christ and accept

---

4. Kyle Snodgrass, *NIV Application Commentary: Ephesians* (Grand Rapids, MI: Zondervan, 1996), 343.
5. Snodgrass, *NIV Application Commentary: Ephesians*, 343.

His redemption, we become His sons and daughters. We are His. The enemy will try at every turn to skew our confidence in our seat at God's table. If we doubt it, he can win. The assurance of our salvation guards our thoughts, reminding us whose we are.

SWORD OF THE SPIRIT

Paul labels the sword of the Spirit as the Word of God. Like the shield of faith, this weapon works both to defend and to advance. In the hands of a person who knows how to wield it, a sword is a powerful weapon. It cuts and mars while clanking against the armaments of the attacker, protecting the one in the fight.

We see Jesus using this very weapon when He encounters the devil in the desert in Matthew 4. At every turn as the enemy tempts Jesus, the Word saturates His response. He fights back with truth written in the Word of God. The Word empowers Jesus to defeat the devil.

In order to truly use this weapon, we must be in the Word, committing to its truth, allowing it to steep in our souls.

PRAY IN THE SPIRIT

The last and final weapon Paul mentions in the list is to pray in the Spirit. He says, "Pray in the Spirit on all occasions with all kinds of prayers and requests . . . be alert and always keep on praying for all the Lord's people" (Ephesians 6:18). Prayer aligns our hearts with God's desires. When we pray in every season, our attitudes adjust and gratitude grows. When we pray for others, our selfishness wanes. Everyone benefits. Prayer brings healing. James tells us "the prayer of a righteous person is powerful and effective" (James 5:16). Prayer changes situations and moves the heart of God. When we have nothing else, we have prayer.

With this armor on, we are called to action. Paul begs us to set our hearts and minds on things above, not on earthly things (Colossians 3:2). This isn't easy. It takes intentional effort. I fail daily, but it doesn't mean I just quit doing it. I fall. I stand back up with the help of my God. I suit up again and again. I admit my flop, lock shields, and go into battle again. The enemy wants to keep us down and out of the game. If he can remove us completely, he's won the fight.

I'd like to introduce you to one more weapon. It's not listed in Scripture, but I'm fairly certain we all have one. It seems unsuspecting as far as weaponry is concerned, but its impact is undeniable.

I think we all have a megaphone. That's right. Those trumpet-like speakers. When we hold this megaphone, we declare the praises of our God and the good tidings of great joy that shall be to all people (Luke 2:10).

Let's use our megaphones right now! Write the following verses below and read them aloud to cement these truths in your heart and mind:

We tell our stories and God's to the world, and we overcome the enemy. (Revelation 12:11)
Write out Revelation 12:11 and read it aloud:

When God holds the megaphone:

He reminds us we are His. (Isaiah 43:1)
Write and read aloud Isaiah 43:1:

He sings over us with delight. (Zephaniah 3:17)

Write and read aloud Zephaniah 3:17:

His words, laced with love, shower strength into a weary warrior. (Isaiah 41:10)

Write and read aloud Isaiah 41:10:

But occasionally something catastrophic happens. We loosen our grip on the megaphone and the enemy grabs it from our hands. He pairs it with his dialect of deceit, accuses us, and serves us a heaping side of shame. This tactic is highly effective at times, especially when we are unaware of whose hands are holding the megaphone at that moment.

As effective as it might be, we can still triumph because we don't fight with the same weapons the enemy does. "The weapons we fight with are not the weapons of the world. On the contrary, they have divine power to demolish strongholds. We demolish arguments and every pretension that sets itself up against the knowledge of God, and we take captive every thought to make it obedient to Christ" (2 Corinthians 10:4–5).

The power to destroy strongholds is available to us. We can obliterate the lies the enemy speaks. No weapon formed against us will prevail, and we will refute every tongue that accuses us (Isaiah 54:17).

You are known, valued, and loved by God. The Creator and Sustainer of the Universe is for you and is on your side. That's a powerful way to win a war.

Read Ephesians 6:10–18 aloud.

What stands out the most?

Which weapon do you use most often and why?

Which weapon do you need to sharpen and why?

When have you noticed the "megaphone" in use lately? Have you noticed it in the wrong hands?

WEEK 2 | DAY 1

MY GOD IS FOR ME

Sometimes I wish I wasn't so trusting. I have a tendency to give a person the benefit of the doubt, only to be disappointed when I realize their motivation is not quite what I thought.

In the story of the very first game of hide and seek, we find the four main characters: God, man, woman, and the enemy (the serpent). Knowing the motivation for each of these characters is of great importance. This week, we are going to focus on two characters in the story: God and the enemy.

God is always for man and woman, working good for both of them. Loving them even in their mess. God is always opposed to the enemy, thwarting the enemy's plans and overcoming him in the end.

The enemy is always against man and woman, working to destroy them both. He is opposed to their good and loves to create more and more mess in their lives. The enemy is always opposed to God, trying in every circumstance to stop His work and end His story.

Today we are going to look at what the Bible says about God's relationship with us and how He is for us. Read aloud the beautiful promises in the Scriptures below.

> This is what the Lord says—your Redeemer, who formed you in the womb: I am the Lord, the Maker of all things, who stretches out the heavens, who spreads out the earth by myself. (Isaiah 44:24)

> "To whom will you compare me? Or who is my equal?" says the Holy One. Lift up your eyes and look to the heavens: Who created all these? He who brings out the starry host one by one, and calls forth each of them by name. Because of his great power and mighty strength, not one of them is missing. (Isaiah 40:25–26)

Look back through the verses above. Circle the names of God and underline His actions.

Our Redeemer, the One who formed us, is the Creator of the universe. He single-handedly stretched out the heavens. This is the God who is for you. The God who has unlimited resources. The One who knows every star by name. The One who cannot compare to any other.

This is what the Creator of the Universe says about you and how He is working on your behalf. Read these verses slowly and underline God's actions:

"But you, Israel, my servant, Jacob, whom I have chosen, you descendants of Abraham my friend, I took you from the ends of the earth, from its farthest corners I called you. I said, 'You are my servant'; I have chosen you and have not rejected you. So do not fear, for I am with you; do not be dismayed, for I am your God. I will strengthen you and help you; I will uphold you with my righteous right hand." (Isaiah 41:8–10)

I will go before you and will level the mountains; I will break down gates of bronze and cut through bars of iron. I will give you hidden treasures, riches stored in secret places, so that you may know that I am the Lord, the God of Israel, who summons you by name. For the sake of Jacob, my servant, of Israel my chosen, I summon you by name and bestow on you a title of honor, though you do not acknowledge me. (Isaiah 45:2–4)

But Zion said, "The Lord has forsaken me, the Lord has forgotten me." "Can a mother forget the baby at her breast and have no compassion on the child she has borne? Though she may forget, I will not forget you! See, I have engraved you on the palms of my hands; your walls are ever before me." (Isaiah 49:14–16)

Be strong and courageous. Do not be afraid or terrified because of them, for the Lord your God goes with you; he will never leave you nor forsake you. The Lord himself goes before you and will be with you; he will never leave you nor forsake you. Do not be afraid; do not be discouraged. (Deuteronomy 31:6, 8)

Then I said to you, "Do not be terrified; do not be afraid of them. The Lord your God, who is going before you, will fight for you, as he did for you in Egypt, before your very eyes, and in the wilderness. There you saw how the Lord your God carried you, as a father carries his son, all the way you went until you reached this place." (Deuteronomy 1:29–31)

You are my strength, I watch for you; you, God, are my fortress, my God on whom I can rely. God will go before me
and will let me gloat over those who slander me. (Psalm 59:9–10)

He shall say: "Hear, Israel: Today you are going into battle against your enemies. Do not be fainthearted or afraid; do not panic or be terrified by them. For the Lord your God is the one who goes with you to fight for you against your enemies to give you victory." (Deuteronomy 20:3–4)

Which of these Scriptures speaks the loudest to you? Why?

Which actions of God stand out the most? Why?

What do you see about the character of God and how He feels toward you? How does this change the game?

Lord Jesus, thank You. Thank You for the way You go before me and fight for me when I cannot fight for myself. Thank You for fighting even when I don't trust You the way I should. I cannot understand why the God of the universe is interested in my everyday, ordinary life. I trust You to make the difference. Help me to stand firm and to cling to the hope of Your cross and Your deliverance. Amen.

WHO DOES GOD SAY I AM?

I had a long and restless night. I was muddling through my personal journey toward grace, struggling to see my worth in Christ. The next morning, I walked into my office to find someone had slipped a small piece of paper under my door. It wasn't signed. It had no note. The paper listed simple statements about "Who I Am in Christ" and the Scripture references to back them up. I glanced at it and honestly didn't spend enough time really letting the truth of each statement soak in.

Since that morning, I've spent many moments looking at this list and asking God to make these statements a part of the person I know He has remade me to be. Along the way, I didn't always believe the truths on the paper, but I asked for God to reveal the truth of them anyway, praying my faith would grow and I would trust His truth more and more.

A big part of fighting and winning the battle with wanting to hide comes in understanding who you *really* are. Knowing you belong to Christ and you are His own child brings a freedom no other truth can.

Take some time today to read through this list of statements and the Scripture references rooting them in truth. Allow these truths to really soak into your soul. Spend some time writing your responses to these truths under "Your Thoughts." Be honest with God. You may be struggling to believe some of them. Tell Him. Ask for help understanding what He says about who you are. Spend time thanking Him for His Word and His truth.

WHO YOU ARE IN CHRIST:

I am a child of God.

He came into the very world he created, but the world didn't recognize him. He came to his own people, and even they rejected him. But to all who believed him and accepted him, he gave the right to become children of God. (John 1:10–12 NLT)

Your Thoughts:

I have been bought with a price. I belong to God.

You do not belong to yourself, for God bought you with a high price. (1 Corinthians 6:19–20 NLT)

Do not be afraid, for I have ransomed you. I have called you by name; you are mine. For I am the Lord, your God, the Holy One of Israel, your Savior. Others were given in exchange for you. I traded their lives for yours because you are precious to me. You are honored, and I love you. (Isaiah 43:1, 3–4 NLT)

Your Thoughts:

I have been adopted as God's child.

Long before he laid down earth's foundations, he had us in mind, had settled on us as the focus of his love, to be made whole and holy by his love. Long, long ago he decided to adopt us into his family through Jesus Christ. (What pleasure he took in planning this!) He wanted us to enter into the celebration of his lavish gift-giving by the hand of his beloved Son. (Ephesians 1:4–6 MSG)

Your Thoughts:

I have been redeemed and forgiven of all my sins.

For he has rescued us from the kingdom of darkness and transferred us into the Kingdom of his dear Son, who purchased our freedom and forgave our sins. (Colossians 1:13–14 NLT)

Your Thoughts:

I am complete in Christ.

For in Christ lives all the fullness of God in a human body. So you also are complete through your union with Christ, who is the head over every ruler and authority. For you were buried with Christ when you were baptized. And with him you were raised to new life because you trusted the mighty power of God, who raised Christ from the dead. (Colossians 2:9, 12 NLT)

Your Thoughts:

I cannot be separated from the love of God.

I am convinced that nothing can ever separate us from God's love. Neither death nor life, neither angels nor demons, neither our fears for today nor our worries about tomorrow—not even the powers of hell can separate us from God's love. No power in the sky above or in the earth below—indeed, nothing in all creation will ever be able to separate us from the love of God that is revealed in Christ Jesus our Lord. (Romans 8:38–39 NLT)

Your Thoughts:

I have not been given a spirit of fear, but a spirit of power, love, and a sound mind.

> For God has not given us a spirit of fear and timidity, but of power, love, and self-discipline. So never be ashamed to tell others about our Lord. . . . With the strength God gives you, be ready to suffer with me for the sake of the Good News. (2 Timothy 1:7–8 NLT)

Your Thoughts:

I am God's workmanship and am wonderfully made.

> For we are God's masterpiece. He has created us anew in Christ Jesus, so we can do the good things he planned for us long ago. (Ephesians 2:10 NLT)

> For you created my inmost being; you knit me together in my mother's womb. I praise you because I am fearfully and wonderfully made; your works are wonderful, I know that full well. My frame was not hidden from you when I was made in the secret place, when I was woven together in the depths of the earth. Your eyes saw my unformed body; all the days ordained for me were written in your book before one of them came to be. (Psalm 139:13–16)

Your Thoughts:

I may approach God with freedom and confidence.

In him and through faith in him we may approach God with freedom and confidence. (Ephesians 3:12 NLT)

For we do not have a high priest who is unable to empathize with our weaknesses, but we have one who has been tempted in every way, just as we are—yet he did not sin. Let us then approach God's throne of grace with confidence, so that we may receive mercy and find grace to help us in our time of need. (Hebrews 4:15–16 NLT)

Your Thoughts:

PRAYER FOR THE DAY

Choose your favorite truth statement and write a prayer thanking God for making it true in you.

WEEK 2 | DAY 3

YOU CAN'T HIDE FROM GOD

Abigail's room was a bit untidy (not an unusual thing), so I helped her pick up a few things. As I removed Bob the Big Old Bear from her bed, I discovered a stash of candy wrappers. Had I not moved Bob, I would have never known they were there. Abigail professed she had absolutely no idea how those got there. Bob doesn't eat candy, so I think it's pretty obvious how they got there. Still, she stood her ground and stubbornly held to her claim.

Hiding from God is a little like that. We can pretend something didn't happen, but He knows the truth. Always.

We're going to uncover some truth about what God sees and knows and how He responds. Today we will be engaging Scripture by listening, lingering, learning, then living. You will read the passage four times with a different focus and set of questions each time.

Today's text is Psalm 139. This text may be familiar. If so, take a moment to ask God to give you fresh eyes as you encounter it today.

LISTEN

Read Psalm 139. It's printed for you in the New International Version below.

Sit quietly for a moment before you begin. Ask the Holy Spirit to speak and show you what the Lord wants for you in this passage. Mark words or phrases that stand out as you read.

> You have searched me, Lord,
>   and you know me.
> You know when I sit and when I rise;
>   you perceive my thoughts from afar.

You discern my going out and my lying down;
  you are familiar with all my ways.
Before a word is on my tongue
  you, Lord, know it completely.
You hem me in behind and before,
  and you lay your hand upon me.
Such knowledge is too wonderful for me,
  too lofty for me to attain.

Where can I go from your Spirit?
  Where can I flee from your presence?
If I go up to the heavens, you are there;
  if I make my bed in the depths, you are there.
If I rise on the wings of the dawn,
  if I settle on the far side of the sea,
even there your hand will guide me,
  your right hand will hold me fast.
If I say, "Surely the darkness will hide me
  and the light become night around me,"
even the darkness will not be dark to you;
  the night will shine like the day,
  for darkness is as light to you.

For you created my inmost being;
  you knit me together in my mother's womb.
I praise you because I am fearfully and wonderfully made;
  your works are wonderful,
  I know that full well.
My frame was not hidden from you
  when I was made in the secret place,
  when I was woven together in the depths of the earth.
Your eyes saw my unformed body;
  all the days ordained for me were written in your book

before one of them came to be.
How precious to me are your thoughts, God!
  How vast is the sum of them!
Were I to count them,
  they would outnumber the grains of sand—
  when I awake, I am still with you.

If only you, God, would slay the wicked!
  Away from me, you who are bloodthirsty!
They speak of you with evil intent;
  your adversaries misuse your name.
Do I not hate those who hate you, Lord,
  and abhor those who are in rebellion against you?
I have nothing but hatred for them;
  I count them my enemies.
Search me, God, and know my heart;
  test me and know my anxious thoughts.
See if there is any offensive way in me,
  and lead me in the way everlasting.

LINGER

Read the passage again out loud. Are the same words or phrases you marked the first time still standing out? Write them down. How do these words or phrases apply to your life right now?

LEARN

As you read the text for a third time, ask yourself, "How is God inviting me to respond? What does He want me to be learning from this?" Write out what comes to mind.

Read the passage one last time and answer these questions:

Why is God showing me this now?

What does this mean for my life?

What needs to change in my life?

How do I need to live differently?

PRAYER FOR THE DAY

Lord Jesus, search me. Show me where I am hiding from You and from others. Show me how You have loved me from the beginning. Teach me to find comfort in Your knowledge of me. Show me how You have loved those around me from the beginning. Lead me in Your everlasting way. Amen.

WHO IS MY ENEMY, REALLY?

Great war commanders study their enemies. They look for patterns in their enemies' tactics, and they strategize accordingly.

Today, we move our focus to another character in the story: the enemy (a.k.a. the serpent, Satan, the devil). So much of the time, we do not talk about the enemy. While he is certainly not the star of the story, he does exist and plays a significant supporting role. Understanding his motivation is crucial to our journey to be found.

Take a look at this list of the translation of the Hebrew and Greek words for the enemy:

opponent	*archenemy*	*adversary*	*enemy*
destroyer	*false accuser*	*slanderer*	*foe*

As you read this list, what do you see? What comes to mind?

Read the passage below from John 10. Notice the difference in the actions of Jesus as the Shepherd and the enemy as the thief and the wolf.

> Therefore Jesus said again, "Very truly I tell you, I am the gate for the sheep. All who have come before me are thieves and robbers, but the sheep have not listened to them. I am the gate; whoever enters through me will be saved. They will come in and go out, and find pasture. The thief comes only to steal and kill and destroy; I have come that they may have life, and have it to the full.
>
> I am the good shepherd. The good shepherd lays down his life for the sheep. The hired hand is not the shepherd and does not own the sheep. So when he sees the wolf coming, he abandons the sheep and runs

away. Then the wolf attacks the flock and scatters it. The man runs away because he is a hired hand and cares nothing for the sheep.

I am the good shepherd; I know my sheep and my sheep know me—just as the Father knows me and I know the Father—and I lay down my life for the sheep. I have other sheep that are not of this sheep pen. I must bring them also. They too will listen to my voice, and there shall be one flock and one shepherd. The reason my Father loves me is that I lay down my life—only to take it up again. No one takes it from me, but I lay it down of my own accord. I have authority to lay it down and authority to take it up again. This command I received from my Father." (John 10:7–18)

Below list the actions of Jesus the Shepherd and the actions of Satan the Thief.

Actions of Jesus the Shepherd	Actions of Satan the Thief

How do the actions of Jesus differ from those of the enemy?

In every situation, the enemy is opposed to the things of God. He is opposed to the best for God's children.

Be alert and of sober mind. Your enemy the devil prowls around like a roaring lion looking for someone to devour. Resist him, standing firm in the faith, because you know that the family of believers throughout the world are undergoing the same kind of sufferings. (1 Peter 5:8–9)

How does understanding these things about your enemy the devil change your perspective?

Knowledge is power. In a battle, you need power to overcome your enemy. Understanding your enemy's strategy helps you in combat. Peter challenges us to be self-controlled and alert when it comes to dealing with the devil.

What does it look like for you to be self-controlled and alert?

Take a moment to write the ways your enemy is currently opposing you. How can you hand those things over to God for Him to fight for you?

PRAYER FOR THE DAY

Lord Jesus, I need You to fight for me. I know You are the Good Shepherd, my protector, and my deliverer. You have fought the fight and You have won. You hold the world in Your hands (Colossians 1:17) and You know my situation. You see how the enemy is opposing me. Open my eyes to see where You are fighting for me. Show me where I am not self-controlled and alert and help me to become more so. Amen.

TAKING BACK THE MEGAPHONE

Sometimes I hear voices.

I know. Not a popular thing to say. In some circles admitting that could be downright dangerous. But it's true. I hear voices all the time. Ones that shout and scream that I'm too fat; wrinkly, old, inexperienced, stupid, shy, stubborn, over-bearing, (insert just about any word here). Voices that say, "She's so much better than you are. You don't matter to them. You can't possibly do that. Because you did *that*, you're not worth anything."

I want to be the kind of woman who "demolishes arguments and every pretention that sets itself up against the knowledge of God, and takes every thought captive and makes it obedient to Christ" (2 Corinthians 10:5). But these voices sometimes keep me from being this kind of woman. The battle rages in our minds. The battle over our thoughts is intense. The struggle is very real, friends.

Remember the megaphone? You have one. I have one. I believe this weapon plays a major role in the violent battle raging over our thoughts. Our megaphone's primary purpose is for us to declare the praise and the glory of God. We use it to broadcast God's story to the world. God also uses it. God sings over us and speaks truth to us, reminding us who and whose we are.

The enemy has an altogether different agenda where the megaphone is concerned. It's not surprising, considering he's not for us and opposes the things of God.

When we struggle to hear God singing over us without rebuke (Zephaniah 3:17), when we loosen our grip on the megaphone, and sometimes when we just aren't being alert, the enemy likes to grab the megaphone and speak lies over us. At times, it's just a faint voice, but sometimes he decides to plug it into a loudspeaker and screech instead.

He says things like, "You're not enough! You'll never be enough! God cannot possibly redeem that! You're of no use here! What would make you think you could do that?" The list goes on and on.

The problem with the enemy holding the megaphone is he's a deceiver. He's a master liar because, on most occasions, his lies contain tiny bits of truth, making it harder to see the lie outright. Maybe we're not being completely honest with God to receive His redemption, and the enemy holds that over us. Maybe we need to work on something a little harder because we've just been lazy, and the enemy says we won't accomplish anything. Maybe we need to *not* do a particular thing because our pride is at the center of doing it, and the enemy murmurs we really are the center.

We are sinful people. True. But we are no longer covered with shame. The enemy no longer gets to speak to what is not his. If you are in Christ, there is *no* condemnation (Romans 8:1). Not even a smidge.

Here is a great prescription for taking back the megaphone:

> A final word: Be strong in the Lord and in his mighty power. Put on all of God's armor so that you will be able to stand firm against all strategies of the devil. For we are not fighting against flesh-and-blood enemies, but against evil rulers and authorities of the unseen world, against mighty powers in this dark world, and against evil spirits in the heavenly places. Therefore, put on every piece of God's armor so you will be able to resist the enemy in the time of evil. Then after the battle you will still be standing firm. Stand your ground, putting on the belt of truth and the body armor of God's righteousness. For shoes, put on the peace that comes from the Good News so that you will be fully prepared. In addition to all of these, hold up the shield of faith to stop the fiery arrows of the devil. Put on salvation as your helmet, and take the sword of the Spirit, which is the word of God. Pray in the Spirit at all times and on every occasion. Stay alert and be persistent in your prayers for all believers everywhere. (Ephesians 6:10–18 NLT)

When has the megaphone been in the wrong hands lately?

What truths will allow you to take back the megaphone?

Go back through Week 2 Day 2 and list some of the truths you need to remember.

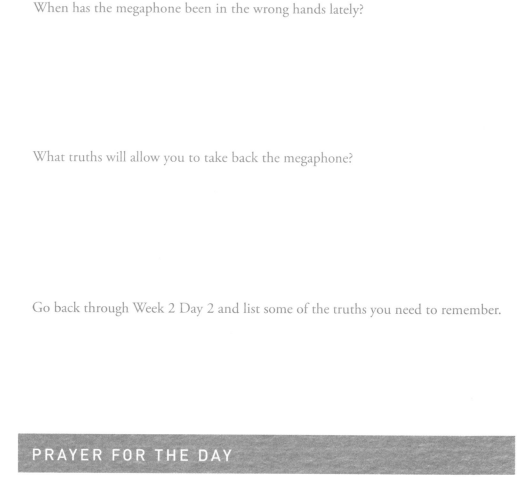

PRAYER FOR THE DAY

Lord Jesus, You are singing over me (Zephaniah 3:17). You have redeemed me and called me Your own (Isaiah 43:1). I belong to You. You have given me worth and value rooted in Your love for me. Open my mind and my heart to see when the enemy is screaming into the megaphone. Give me the strength to take it back with the armor You have provided. Remind me of the truth in Your Word and help me to speak it in times when I have no other strength. Your belt of truth covers me, and Your sword gives me a defense. Thank you for not leaving me defenseless. Amen.

TRUTH, LIES, AND ACTION

Throughout this week we've been exchanging lies for truth, so it's no surprise that we should wrap up the week with Truth, Lies, and Action. Here's a reminder:

TRUTH: A new way of looking at a truth from God's Word to replace the →
LIES: We want to name the lies we've believed and reclaim them with new truths to move us into →
ACTION: Because faith without works is dead (James 2:20), we want to be people of action. We will be looking today and tomorrow at specific action steps we can take to come out of hiding.

Perhaps this exercise will have a whole new meaning this time around, having studied the importance of trading truth for the lies in the battle.

TRUTH: Our first memory verse says:

> But now, this is what the Lord says—he who created you, Jacob, he who formed you, Israel: "Do not fear, for I have redeemed you; I have summoned you by name; you are mine." (Isaiah 43:1)

TRUTH tells us we now belong to the God who created us because He has redeemed us—we are His.

TRUTH also tells us we have an enemy who is very real and is constantly looking for ways to completely destroy us.

> Be alert and of sober mind. Your enemy the devil prowls around like a roaring lion looking for someone to devour. (1 Peter 5:8)

What other truths did you discover this week?

LIES: The LIE tells us many things. It tells us God can't possibly love us because of what we've thought, how we've felt, or what we've done. It tells us we are not accepted by God when we are, in fact, redeemed and belong to Him.

What other lies did you discover this week?

ACTION: Over the next few days, consider one of these action steps to help you take back the megaphone and come out of hiding:

- Find one trustworthy friend and share something you learned about yourself this week.
- Do you need to tell someone something but you've been putting it off because of shame? Find the person and share what you've been withholding.
- Make a list of the common lies the enemy speaks through your megaphone. Make a list of Scriptures to help you fill your armory and allow you to combat the lies the enemy tries to speak over you.
- Take some time to write out the Scriptures from Day 2 you most need to hear. Put them in a prominent place to remind you that you belong to the Creator of the universe.

Write about your ACTION step below. Share why you chose it and what the results were.

Lord Jesus, thank You for redeeming me—for claiming me as Your own even when I feel unworthy. I pray You will allow me to stand firm and resist the enemy. Show me clearly when he is trying to gain ground belonging to You. I don't want to run from You anymore. Help me to stand before You in my depraved state and to allow Your grace to wash over me again and again. Show me how You have loved me. Amen.

come out, come

out,
wherever
you are!

God saved you by his grace when you believed. And you can't take credit for this; it is a gift from God. Salvation is not a reward for the good things we have done, so none of us can boast about it. For we are God's masterpiece. He has created us anew in Christ Jesus, so we can do the good things he planned for us long ago. **EPHESIANS 2:8–10 NLT**

We are beginning week three, and this week we hope to peel back the layers you've been hiding behind. It may be a little painful at first, but I pray, in time, you will see the beauty of emerging from the shell you've built around yourself. May God guide you through this week's study as He reminds you He loves you deeply and will never leave you or forsake you.

INTRODUCTION TO WEEK 3

WHY DO YOU REALLY HIDE?

I'm not sure when it started. The timeline of my childhood memories blurs, so I rely on what I've been told. My parents have always said I sang before I talked. The melodies of "Shop Around" and "Sunshine on My Shoulders" crossed my two-year-old lips frequently.

I perfected the art of performing at an early age. I learned how to put on a show. I mastered the skill of becoming someone else to earn the approval and love of those in the audience. If I feared belonging, I impersonated someone who would belong. If someone had expectations, I not only met them, I *exceeded* them to make sure the person would be pleased—and I wouldn't be rejected.

After decades of operating this way, a significant problem arose: I couldn't keep up with the circus act. Living this way requires enormous effort and a ton of work. It exhausts a person. I grew weary, unable to meet the expectations. Working so hard to belong and then not fitting in drained me.

Fear settled in. I wanted so much to just step off the stage and drop the act, but I wondered if I would ever be enough. Would anyone ever accept me? If people knew the *real* me, how would they ever love me?

> *This God is for you.* This all-powerful deity who shows His splendor in all of creation is for you.

Fear shackles shame. Fear shines a spotlight on shame, saying, "Dance!" All of us long to be fully known. To be told we have value. To be loved as we are. We fear it will never happen. It's something we don't advertise outright because that would just be plain crazy. So instead, we parade around, silently begging for the approval of others while we do our song and dance, all the while fearing we will never be known, valued, and loved at all. So we sing. And dance. And parade around.

God made a way for us to step off the stage. We no longer have to live afraid. The only thing we are to fear is God Himself. What does it really mean to fear God? In the English language, fear causes distress and anxiety. It points to danger, evil, and threats, whether real or imagined. First Chronicles 16:25 says the Lord is great, most worthy of praise, and to be feared above all gods. The essence of the word "feared" in the Hebrew is different than our understanding of fear. The Hebrew word *yare'* says we will stand in awe of God and have a deep reverence and respect for Him. The passage goes on to share the mighty nature of God, showing the kinds of acts that allow for this kind of response to an amazing God. He controls all we see and governs all we don't see. We could have much to fear about God, but our fear is to be a reverence, an awe, a wonder of all He is—not a fear of punishment from His hand.

This God is for you. This all-powerful deity who shows His splendor in all of creation is for you. He proved He was for you when He sent His one and only Son to die for your sins (John 3:16). When Jesus put on flesh and joined humanity, He verified He is for you. When He willingly went to the cross and gave His flesh to right the wrongs we have done, He confirmed His deep love for you and for me.

Psalm 27:1 says, "The Lord is my light and my salvation—whom shall I fear? The Lord is the stronghold of my life—of whom shall I be afraid?" With *this* kind of God—a God who gave His life for you—on your side, you don't need to fear.

Yet, we still struggle with fear. We still wrestle with belonging. We still fear we aren't enough and never will be. We still grapple with putting forth enough effort to be valuable in God's eyes, as though we have to earn His love. Shame shouts, "It's impossible for us to be loved in our broken state," and we believe it. We may believe God knows us, but it's difficult to imagine God knowing us and loving us anyway. It seems too good to be true.

Our culture seems to uphold those beliefs. Our system of economics says we should get what we deserve, be paid whatever wages we have earned. Romans tells us we have earned death because of our sin (Romans 6:23). Our shame proves the death we deserve to die. This is where God's economy differs from ours. He exchanges the life of His Son simply because of the worth He sees in us, because of His love for us. Christ demonstrates His love for us by dying in a heinous manner while we are still sinners (Romans 5:8). He went to the cross knowing we would choose sin. Love held Him there. Understanding why He would do it is difficult. I don't love that way. I don't really know anyone who loves that way. But God does.

God gave us a gift of grace, unmerited favor. We do not deserve the forgiveness or the acceptance, but God gives it anyway. We are saved by His grace, not by anything we have ever done (Ephesians 2:8). *Nothing* we can do will ever erase our sin and shame. Our sin can be covered only by the blood of Christ.

We regularly confuse God's level of love, acceptance, and forgiveness toward us with our rate of growth as we come to look more like Jesus. We misunderstand, thinking they are somehow dependent upon one another. They are not. This mix-up leads to confusion and prevents us from understanding how God loves us.

Take a look at this explanation:[6]

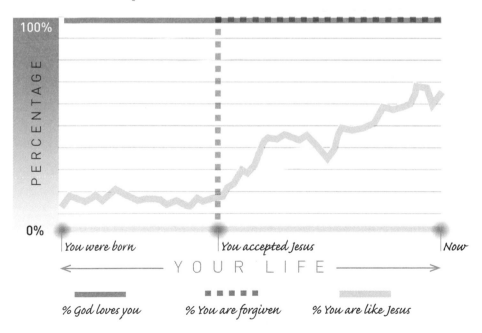

6. I was first introduced to the "Double Cure" by Jack Cottrell at Cincinnati Christian University in my Doctrine of Grace seminary course. This concept helped me on my journey toward grace.

Notice the line measuring God's love for us. Before you were born, God knit you together (Psalm 139). When He formed you, He loved you. Before you were even born. Before you took a breath. Before you sinned and then when you did. There is nothing you could ever do to make God love you more. There is nothing you could ever do to make God love you less. Ever. That line is nonnegotiable. It's not up to us. It originates with a loving, gracious Father and is truly unconditional.

God loves us, but with sin, a great chasm was forged. Our Holy God cannot be in the presence of sin. We needed something—Someone—to bridge the divide between a sinful people and a Holy God. We needed a cure. A cure that is two-fold is what God provides—*a double cure.*

First of all, we needed to be forgiven. Our sins erased. Examine the line calculating our level of forgiveness. When we choose Jesus as Savior, we jump from the 0 percent mark on the forgiven scale to the 100 percent mark on the scale—no stops along the way. The shift is drastic and radical. This forgiveness is possible only because of the cross. There is no condemnation for those in Christ, only forgiveness, acceptance, love (Romans 8:1). His work on the cross takes away our sin and shame. Period. Nothing is required on our part to receive forgiveness other than confessing we are sinners in need of a Savior and choosing to accept the gift of grace Jesus offers. His pain covers our shame. Completely.

Second, God wants to grow and change us. He longs for us to be formed into the image of Jesus. This line, though, is one we often mistake for God's love and acceptance of us. It is the gradual, slow process moving us from our sinful state to looking more like Jesus. This line is called *sanctification*, or the process of becoming holy—becoming more like Christ.

When we measure our worth based on this line, we flirt with disaster. If we are moving in the right direction, we begin to think we are somehow more valuable than someone who might not be as far along as we are. We judge them, elevating our own worth. The opposite is also true. We believe if others are further along in the journey or are making better time, then we are somehow less valuable to God.

Neither of these is true, and both are playgrounds for shame. Becoming more like Jesus is a slow journey with ups and downs. You can take steps forward and just as quickly spiral down again. All of us struggle in it. Sometimes we do it well, and other times, not so much. Basing our value and worth on this line will prove uncertain every time.

Sin is separation from God. Whatever your sin is, it separates you from God. God has no degrees of separation based on your offense; every single sin ever committed requires the exact same price to redeem it. No sin is exempt from needing the blood of Jesus to restore it. The same covering is required for us all.

Just as in the beginning when sin entered, God made a sacrifice and a covering. Jesus gave His life for you to cover you and remove completely the shame of your sin, once and for all (Hebrews 10:10). When we believe it takes our work and effort to earn God's love, we begin to believe we had something to do with our redemption. "God saved you by his grace when you believed. And you can't take credit for this; it is a gift from God. Salvation is not a reward for the good things we have done, so none of us can boast about it" (Ephesians 2:8–9 NLT). We cannot take credit for the grace we've been shown. God gifted grace. It's not a reward for good behavior. If it were, you better believe we'd all be thinking more about how great our performance was instead of how remarkable our God is. He is the source of it all. We are the recipients of the gift.

You don't have to perform anymore. You can come out, come out, wherever you are. Just as you are. Grace is yours. You are forgiven. You are seen, known, and deeply loved by the Creator of the universe. You are free.

LINGER AND LEARN

Read Ephesians 2:8–10.

How does the "Double Cure" change your view of the way God loves and forgives you?

How has not being enough caused you to hide?

What would it take for you to believe God sees you as enough already?

I AM SAVED BY GRACE

On my desk at work, I have a framed chalkboard on which I had planned to write different Scriptures. I had every intention of changing the verses periodically depending on what I felt God was trying to teach me in the moment. But the same Scripture has been on it for the past two years—since the day I first came up with this idea. Let's just say God has been trying to teach me this one for some time now.

One of the ways I have tried to hide has been attempting to do things to win the favor and approval of others, also known as "perfectionism." I find it interesting when people say, "Oh, well, I'm definitely not a perfectionist. You should see how messy my house is!" or "I am not a perfectionist. I never wear any makeup and rarely look like I have it together!"

I love Brené Brown's definition of perfection from her book *Daring Greatly*. She says, "Perfectionism is not the same thing as striving for excellence. Perfectionism is not about healthy achievement and growth. Perfectionism is a defensive move. It's the belief that if we do things perfectly and look perfect, we can minimize or avoid the pain of blame, judgment, and shame. Perfectionism is a twenty-ton shield that we lug around, thinking it will protect us, when in fact it's the thing that's really preventing us from being seen."[7]

We may not like the word "perfectionism," but I think we all find a little of ourselves in that definition. Most of us, at some level, are concerned about managing the image others have of us. We are concerned about whether or not certain people "approve" of what we are doing and accomplishing—or at the very least, how we are performing. A while ago, I was introduced to a concept that changed the way I was thinking about this challenge. It's called the "Cycle of Works."[8]

---

7. Brené Brown, *Daring Greatly: How the Courage to Be Vulnerable Transforms the Way We Live, Love, Parent, and Lead*, (New York, NY: Gotham Books, 2012), 128–29.
8. Cycle of Works/Cycle of Grace adapted from Dr. Frank Lake's *Clinical Theology* by Eddie Gibbs. I was introduced to this beautiful mess by Sibyl Towner, my mentor. It initially wrecked me. Now it has given me a tangible understanding of Ephesians 2:8–10.

In this "Cycle of Works," you begin at the top left corner of the wheel:

1. You achieve something. You accomplish something through your own effort. Which leads to number 2.
2. You find significance. Because you have accomplished something, you feel significant. Which leads to number 3.
3. You have sustaining strength. Because you feel significant, you find sustaining strength—for as long as the accomplishment lasts. Which leads to number 4.
4. You are accepted. By God, by others. Because you have accomplished something and you have significance and sustaining strength, you are accepted and loved.

Most of us live in this never-ending cycle. It works, but it has many problems. For starters, your worth and acceptance last only as long as the memory of your accomplishment. Other people will accomplish many things you cannot begin to do, or they will accomplish things you can do in a much better way and with greater ease. People will quickly forget what is so great about whatever it is you achieved. Because of this, you will be driven faster and faster around the wheel. You will have to work harder and better in order to make it around the wheel quickly before your accomplishment wears off.

This is exhausting. Trust me. I know.

But this is a way we hide. We hide behind our accomplishments and achievements like a shield, hoping people will see them instead of us, instead of our failures, instead of our real selves. But we can't keep up with this version of the wheel. It just can't happen. And the more we try, the more likely we are to end up having some sort of breakdown that may or may not include insomnia, depression, anxiety, fatigue, and other potential side effects. It's just not worth it.

But there is another way.

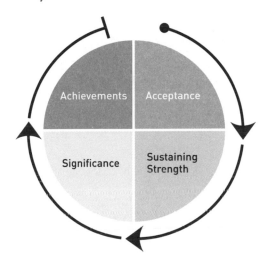

If you begin in the top right corner of the wheel at "acceptance," you'll see the "Cycle of Grace."

1. You are accepted and loved by God. That is all. Because He made you and He says you are loved. No arguing. Which leads to number 2.
2. You have sustaining strength. The Creator of the universe loves you beyond measure. He delights in you, and His love brings an unmatched strength. Which leads to number 3.
3. You are significant. The Creator of the universe loves you beyond measure and created you with a specific purpose. He is for you. You belong to Him. He has a plan for your life. Nothing can possibly bring more significance. Which leads to number 4.
4. As a result of this amazing love, you want to achieve something to bring God glory.

And you're done. One time around. That. Is. All. No spinning around the wheel. No seeing how fast you can get around the cycle again so the acceptance doesn't wear off. It simply won't. God's love and acceptance for you will NOT run out.

This cycle beautifully demonstrates the truth in Ephesians 2—which happens to be what is written on the board on my desk in my office.

Read aloud Ephesians 2:1–10 from the New Living Translation. Pray that God cements these truths in your heart and mind:

> Once you were dead because of your disobedience and your many sins. You used to live in sin, just like the rest of the world, obeying the devil— the commander of the powers in the unseen world. He is the spirit at work in the hearts of those who refuse to obey God. All of us used to live that way, following the passionate desires and inclinations of our sinful nature. By our very nature we were subject to God's anger, just like everyone else.
>
> But God is so rich in mercy, and he loved us so much, that even though we were dead because of our sins, he gave us life when he raised Christ from the dead. (It is only by God's grace that you have been saved!) For he raised us from the dead along with Christ and seated us with him in the heavenly realms because we are united with Christ Jesus. So God can point to us in all future ages as examples of the incredible wealth of his grace and kindness toward us, as shown in all he has done for us who are united with Christ Jesus.
>
> God saved you by his grace when you believed. And you can't take credit for this; it is a gift from God. Salvation is not a reward for the good things we have done, so none of us can boast about it. For we are God's masterpiece. He has created us anew in Christ Jesus, so we can do the good things he planned for us long ago.

Go back and underline the sentence beginning with "And you can't take credit for this." Reread that sentence and the next.

I can't take credit for this. You can't take credit for this. God does not give salvation—or anything, for that matter—in exchange for the good things we have done. Our work earns us *squat*. I love the way author Heather Holleman describes this: "When we're seated with Christ, the difference is that Jesus is with us, and we are looking at our sin together. He is giving us power to change. He isn't shaking His finger or turning His face away when we come to Him with a repentant heart. He's ready to embrace us in the midst of our sin. He loves me. He loves you. He delights in us. We are seated in this delight and acceptance."[9] Seated. The work is finished. We're not looking for a seat at the table anymore.

You were created as a masterpiece, loved and accepted by God. That's right: you are known, valued, and loved by God *because* He created you. You are made clean, are accepted, and have a secure seat at the table because of the work of Jesus on the cross. Because you have been made new and because He crafted you to do them, you accomplish *good things* planned for you long ago.

What do you need to remember about the "Cycle of Works/Cycle of Grace"?

How does Ephesians 2:1–10 speak to you today?

9. Heather Holleman, *Seated with Christ: Living Freely in a Culture of Comparison* (Chicago: Moody, 2015), 134.

What is God calling you to do differently as a result of these truths?

How does understanding this Scripture and the Cycle of Works/Cycle of Grace help you come out of hiding?

PRAYER FOR THE DAY

Lord Jesus, You have loved me from my beginning. I have a hard time accepting I am Your masterpiece, but I trust You to show me that I am. Thank You for creating me to do good things to further Your kingdom. Forgive me for when I have made my good things a part of my salvation process. Thank You for extending grace, even to me. Amen.

I WILL LAY DOWN MY PRIDE

We all have it. We're born with it. It's not something we like to admit possessing ourselves, but we can quickly identify it in others. You'd think it would be easier to own, knowing it's a struggle for everyone, but the nature of it simply won't allow us to live that way.

It's called *pride*.

It can be ugly. It can be deceiving. If it goes undetected, it can be dangerous. The dictionary definition explains pride as a high opinion of one's own dignity—"look at me"; a sense of what is due to oneself or one's position or character; "I should be treated differently"; pleasure or satisfaction taken in something done by or belonging to oneself or believed to reflect credit to oneself. In other words, "Look what I did or what I can do."[10] Each of us may not display all these characteristics at the same time (although I admit I've done it before), but we live in this conflict because of the flesh we wear.

Pride definitely goes before a fall (Proverbs 16:18). Self-importance is rich soil for the root of our sinful and egocentric nature. If we are not aware of our pride, it lurks in the darkness and will leap upon us at inopportune times and when we least expect it.

A biblical king had a serious problem with pride. In 2 Chronicles 26, we find the story of Uzziah, king of Judah. This king is the very same Uzziah mentioned in Isaiah 6 when Isaiah has his vision of the Lord and receives the call to prophesy.

Take a moment to read the story of Uzziah in 2 Chronicles 26.

Uzziah was a mere sixteen years old when he became king of Judah. I'm pretty sure if someone had made me king when I was sixteen, I would have thought I was

---

10. Pride. Dictionary.com. Unabridged. Random House, Inc. http://dictionary.reference.com/browse/pride.

something. But Uzziah was a different kind of kid. "He did what was right in the eyes of the Lord, just as his father Amaziah had done. He sought God during the days of Zechariah, who instructed him in the fear of God. As long as he sought the Lord, God gave him success" (2 Chronicles 26:4–5).

Uzziah sought the Lord, and the Lord gave him success. Uzziah rebuilt the cities and restored Judah after destruction had come upon them. He built many important structures to protect Judah from its enemies. He had a well-trained army ready for battle—307,500 men, to be exact (verse 13). Not only were they well-trained, they were well-equipped with shields, spears, helmets, coats of armor, bows, and slingstones for each man. He even made machines for their war efforts. As a result of all of this, "his fame spread far and wide, for he was greatly helped until he became powerful" (verse15b).

Uzziah sought the Lord and did what was right in His eyes. In return, God gave him significant success. He was famous. And then something happened in Uzziah. Something that happens to the best of us: "But after Uzziah became powerful, his pride led to his downfall. He was unfaithful to the Lord his God, and entered the temple of the Lord to burn incense on the altar of incense" (verse 16).

Uzziah began to think *he* had created the fame that followed him. He started to believe that what *he* had done had brought about his success and renown. Uzziah thought *he* had earned this fame all on his own. He took credit for it.

> When pride is present, we also judge others. We look at our own sin in comparison to those who we feel have sinned in greater ways than we have and we elevate ourselves.

As a result, he thought more highly of himself than he ought. He thought he had somehow earned the right to enter into the presence of the Most Holy God by his own merit. He entered the temple of the Lord to burn his own incense on the altar. This one act of irreverence cost him everything. You see, the priests were the only ones who were allowed to enter this area of the temple. They were the ones who were set apart to enter in and offer a sacrifice on behalf of the people. They were consecrated, accepted in this space, and there were rules about how and when they were even to enter. Uzziah was not a priest, but because of his pride, he felt as though he had earned the right to enter and offer his own sacrifice.

When he was confronted about his choice to enter the temple, Uzziah became argumentative. Almost immediately after his raging outburst, the Lord struck him with leprosy. Leprosy was (and is) a horrible disease considered "unclean." Those who had leprosy were relegated to live isolated lives. Many considered leprosy to be a result of a sin issue with the person who was afflicted. "King Uzziah had leprosy until the day he died. He lived in a separate house—leprous, and banned from the temple of the Lord" (verse 21a).

King Uzziah's leprosy forced him to be separated from everyone from the moment his pride became his downfall. He made a choice—allowing his pride to lead—and it changed the course of his life forever.

The interesting fact about where Uzziah's pride led him is he thought he was entitled to be in the presence of the Lord—to offer his own sacrifice.

Can this be said of us?
When was the last time you really thought about the fact you are able to enter into worship because of the sacrifice of Jesus Christ? Have you ever flippantly entered into worship without thinking about the cost required for you to even be in the presence of the Lord?

When we feel entitled, pride is present. When we are prideful, a downfall is waiting to happen. Pride can keep us hidden from others because we think we don't need a rescuer. It's as though we think we have it all together and don't possibly have anything to hide.

When pride is present, we also judge others. We look at our own sin in comparison to those who we feel have sinned in greater ways than we have and we elevate ourselves. In doing so, we keep others from truly being found.

Fortunately for all of us, God has abundant grace, even for the prideful who do not think they need it.

How and where does your pride show up?

Can you relate to the story of Uzziah? How?

How is God calling you to humility? What would that look like in your life?

Take a moment to remember the sacrifice that allows you to be in the presence of Holy God. Write a prayer of thanks in response.

PRAYER FOR THE DAY

Lord Jesus, help me to remember the price You paid for my life, the price You paid for me to enter the Most Holy Place and stand before God the Father without blemish or defect. You are amazing. Help me never forget what You have saved me from. Remind me I also need to be saved from my own self-righteousness. I know I cannot save myself. I am grateful Your arm is not too short to save (Isaiah 59:1). Amen.

I WILL NOT FEAR

I love a good Broadway refrain. Whether I have the privilege of listening to one or the pleasure of belting it out myself, I enjoy a good show tune. One of my favorites is a song called "I'm Not Afraid of Anything" from Jason Robert Brown's *Songs for a New World.* The character, known only as Woman 1, discloses a catalog of fears belonging to the many people in her life, all the while trying to convince herself she has no fears of her own. By the end of the song, the listener discovers she is dreadfully afraid of not being known or loved.

I remember hearing this song for the first time and noticing the singer's resolve to convince the listener, and herself in the process, that she fears nothing. I think we've all done this. I've done it. I've walked around quipping, "I'm not afraid of anything!" out loud, all the while trembling from fear and anxiety inside. I fear the future and what may or may not happen to my family. I fear what others think of me and if they will still love me when they get to know me. I fear being inadequate and becoming useless and disposable. We all struggle with fear, so we hide it all.

Fear and hiding are inextricably linked. You feel one, so you do the other—they walk hand in hand almost every time. But Scripture tells us we have only one place we are to hide and only one thing we are to fear:

> God is a safe place to hide, ready to help when we need him.
> We stand fearless at the cliff-edge of doom, courageous in seastorm and earthquake. Before the rush and roar of oceans, the tremors that shift mountains. Jacob-wrestling God fights for us, God-of-Angel-Armies protects us. (Psalm 46:1–3 MSG)

> Do not call conspiracy everything this people calls a conspiracy; do not fear what they fear, and do not dread it. The Lord Almighty is the one you are to regard as holy, he is the one you are to fear, he is the one you are to dread. (Isaiah 8:12–13)

God is a safe place to hide. He is the only thing we are to fear. Yet, most of the time, we hide in other places and we fear other things. We fear what others may think of us, or we think they may not accept us if they know the truth about who we are.

Defining the difference between these two types of fear is important. The fear of God refers to a reverential awe—a respect, an understanding of the power God possesses with an equal appreciation of His great love for His children. The fear of man refers to "a distressing emotion aroused by impending danger, evil, pain, etc., whether the threat is real or imagined."[11] Real or imagined. True or perceived. Sometimes the fear I face is false. It's not even based on reality. Our enemy prides himself in this kind of panic and anxiety. Remember, he is the author of lies.

With these different definitions in mind, let me introduce you to a simple Bible study method: the SOAP method. This method can be used for any Scripture to find nuggets of truth to transform us:

S for Scripture: Read slowly through the Scripture.

O for Observations: What are your observations about the text? What do you notice? What stands out?

A for Application: How is God calling you to apply the truth in this Scripture to your life right now? What is He calling you to change? How is He inviting you to be different?

P for Prayer: What can you pray as a result of what God is calling you to do in this passage? What do you need to praise God for or request of Him in response?

Let's use this method to read and study Psalm 27:

11. "Fear." Dictionary.com. Collins English Dictionary—Complete & Unabridged 10th Edition. HarperCollins Publishers. http://dictionary.reference.com/browse/fear.

S for Scripture:

Read slowly through the Scripture:

> The Lord is my light and my salvation—
>   whom shall I fear?
> The Lord is the stronghold of my life—
>   of whom shall I be afraid?
>
> When the wicked advance against me
>   to devour me,
> it is my enemies and my foes
>   who will stumble and fall.
> Though an army besiege me,
>   my heart will not fear;
> though war break out against me,
>   even then I will be confident.
>
> One thing I ask from the Lord,
>   this only do I seek:
> that I may dwell in the house of the Lord
>   all the days of my life,
> to gaze on the beauty of the Lord
>   and to seek him in his temple.
> For in the day of trouble
>   he will keep me safe in his dwelling;
> he will hide me in the shelter of his sacred tent
>   and set me high upon a rock.
>
> Then my head will be exalted
>   above the enemies who surround me;
> at his sacred tent I will sacrifice with shouts of joy;
>   I will sing and make music to the Lord.

Hear my voice when I call, Lord;
  be merciful to me and answer me.
My heart says of you, "Seek his face!"
  Your face, Lord, I will seek.
 Do not hide your face from me,
  do not turn your servant away in anger;
  you have been my helper.
Do not reject me or forsake me,
  God my Savior.
Though my father and mother forsake me,
  the Lord will receive me.
Teach me your way, Lord;
  lead me in a straight path
  because of my oppressors.
Do not turn me over to the desire of my foes,
  for false witnesses rise up against me,
  spouting malicious accusations.

I remain confident of this:
  I will see the goodness of the Lord
  in the land of the living.
Wait for the Lord;
  be strong and take heart
  and wait for the Lord. (Psalm 27 NIV)

O for Observations:

What are your observations about the text? What do you notice? What stands out?
Feel free to underline, circle, highlight within the text.

A for Application:

How is God calling you to apply the truth in this Scripture to your life right now? What is He calling you to change? How is He inviting you to be different?

P for Prayer:

What can you pray as a result of what God is calling you to do in this passage? What do you need to praise God for or request of Him in response? Write your prayer in the space below:

I WILL FORGIVE

I remember the day with clarity: a cool September morning, the trees bursting with color. My husband, Matt, was on a break from school, and we were snoozing, enjoying an agenda-less morning. Then the doorbell rang.

Matt opened the door to two FBI agents. Mulder and Sculley stood in our door-way and asked if they could come in to discuss our adoption with a woman from Russia. You see, we had been struggling with infertility and had recently been approached by a woman offering to help us adopt a child from a Russian hospital. She was helping five couples. The weeks prior to our visit from the agents were a whirlwind. Meetings and papers, money exchanged, promises broken and more made. But we prayed desperately for a child, and it seemed as though God was going to give us one.

As we sat at our tiny kitchen table with the FBI agents asking questions, the only real phrase I remember hearing over and over again was this: "At this time there is no evidence there are any babies."

And there weren't. There never were. We prepared a nursery and our hearts for a baby who didn't exist. The child we longed for wasn't coming. We discovered the photo we'd been praying over was a baby picture of one of this woman's own daughters who was now a young woman. And here we were, in the middle of a federal case.

I was angry. Hurt. I couldn't understand what would cause a person to wound others so deeply. It was pure evil. She did it all on purpose. Our loss for her own personal gain. Matt and I both spiraled into depression, searching for answers and begging God to heal our demolished dreams.

A few months after our visit with the FBI, God showed me something that was hard to grasp. He reminded me people without Him cannot possibly live like

Him. I needed to forgive this woman for the pain she inflicted on our family. My favorite story of forgiveness (besides Jesus on the cross, of course) is the story of Joseph and his brothers found in Genesis 37–50 (if you're not familiar with this story, it's a great narrative, well worth reading). It's an extraordinary story of drama and intrigue, for sure. Joseph's brothers were ruthless. They sold him into slavery, and he walked a very hard road as a result. All the while, God was with Joseph. Even in his trouble, God carried him. Joseph forgave his brothers and was somehow able to see how God used him in mighty ways despite his circumstances.

God is not bound by our past or our present. He determines our future and uses our murky past to somehow free us, no matter what our story is. It's an amazing thing I just don't quite understand.

The most powerful words Joseph spoke to his brothers are found in Genesis 50:20. They thought he had died years before and didn't recognize him in his Egyptian garb, a figure of power. He had just revealed his identity to his brothers and stood before them, having access to the food they had traveled to Egypt for during a famine in their home country. He held the power in his hands, and his response is unbelievable:

> But Joseph said to them, "Don't be afraid. Am I in the place of God? You intended to harm me, but God intended it for good to accomplish what is now being done, the saving of many lives." (Genesis 50:19–20)

Like Joseph, God used the disappointing adoption to teach Matt and me something significant. He revealed our deep desire to be parents and removed the parameters we had set that limited how God could show up. He used the situation for our good.

How have you seen God use something for good someone else intended clearly for harm?

Unforgiveness keeps us in hiding. When we hold tight to anger over certain situations, bitter roots grow and fester, making it difficult to forgive. When we don't let go of the pain in our past, it causes us to hide even more.

Forgiveness is not an easy road. Depending on what has happened in your life, you may need significant time to forgive as well as additional help in pursuing forgiveness. Maybe, though, there is just a small root of unforgiveness plaguing you.[12] With all of this in mind, use the SOAP method of Bible reading to study the following passage.

S for Scripture:
Read slowly through the Scripture:

> Love must be sincere. Hate what is evil; cling to what is good. Be devoted to one another in love. Honor one another above yourselves. Never be lacking in zeal, but keep your spiritual fervor, serving the Lord. Be joyful in hope, patient in affliction, faithful in prayer. Share with the Lord's people who are in need. Practice hospitality.
>
> Bless those who persecute you; bless and do not curse. Rejoice with those who rejoice; mourn with those who mourn. Live in harmony with one another. Do not be proud, but be willing to associate with people of low position. Do not be conceited.
>
> Do not repay anyone evil for evil. Be careful to do what is right in the eyes of everyone. If it is possible, as far as it depends on you, live at peace with everyone. Do not take revenge, my dear friends, but leave room for God's wrath, for it is written: "It is mine to avenge; I will repay," says the Lord. On the contrary: "If your enemy is hungry, feed him; if he is thirsty, give him something to drink.
> In doing this, you will heap burning coals on his head." Do not be overcome by evil, but overcome evil with good. (Romans 12:9–21)

12. If you are searching for additional material on forgiveness, I highly recommend *Choosing Forgiveness* by Nancy DeMoss Wolgemuth and *An Unburdened Heart* by Suzie Eller.

O for Observations:

What are your observations about the text? What do you notice? What stands out?

A for Application:

How is God calling you to apply the truth in this Scripture to your life right now? What is He calling you to change? How is He inviting you to be different?

P for Prayer:

What can you pray as a result of what God is calling you to do in this passage? What do you need to praise God for or request of Him in response? Write your prayer in the space below:

I WILL TRUST IN YOU, LORD

"Just jump. Mommy will catch you. I promise." I assured Abigail as her chubby feet gripped the side of the pool. Her eyes wide with fear, she closed them, bent her little legs, and leaped from the ledge. I grabbed her almost as soon as she jumped. She grinned from ear to ear, begging to do it again.

Trust is a tricky thing. The more others hurt us, the harder trust is. It's also a word thrown around quite a bit without understanding the many facets of it. Trust has four main definitions—three in our English dictionary and one in Hebrew—that matter in our relationships with God and with others:

1. The first dictionary definition is, "a reliance on the integrity, strength, ability, surety, of a person or thing."[13] In other words, confidence in a person's aptitude and whether or not he or she is a sure thing. This kind of trust is typically built over time as we see a person's strength and capacity emerge.

2. The second definition has to do with hope, a "confident expectation of something."[14] We trust or hope something will happen. Sometimes this is in regard to a specific event, but when dealing with our relationships, it can be an expectation or hope someone will respond a certain way.

3. The third description is simply, "a person on whom or a thing on which one relies."[15] When we sit on a chair, we rely on it to hold us. When we enter a relationship, we rely on the person to not hurt us. We trust others to do what they say they will do. But chairs break sometimes and people let us down, which makes building this kind of trust easy at first, but as we see the nature of people, trust becomes complicated.

---

13. Trust. Dictionary.com. Dictionary.com Unabridged. Random House, Inc. http://dictionary.reference.com/browse/trust.
14. Ibid.
15. Ibid.

4. The Hebrew word for trust is *batach* or *betach*. It means to have confidence, to be confident, bold, secure, to be safe, to be assured.[16]

Take that in: safe and secure. Bold and confident.

Trust takes center stage in our journey to come out of hiding. Trusting God to love us the way He says He will helps open the door for us to emerge, to allow ourselves to be seen and known.

Today we will be engaging Scripture by listening, lingering, learning, then living. Read the passage four times with a different focus and set of questions each time. Today's text is Psalm 143.

LISTEN

Read Psalm 143:1–10. Sit quietly for a moment before you begin. Ask the Holy Spirit to speak and show you what the Lord wants for you in this passage. Mark words or phrases that stand out as you read.

> Lord, hear my prayer,
>   listen to my cry for mercy;
> in your faithfulness and righteousness
>   come to my relief.
> Do not bring your servant into judgment,
>   for no one living is righteous before you.
> The enemy pursues me,
>   he crushes me to the ground;
> he makes me dwell in the darkness
>   like those long dead.
> So my spirit grows faint within me;
>   my heart within me is dismayed.
> I remember the days of long ago;
>   I meditate on all your works
>   and consider what your hands have done.

16. James Strong, *A Concise Dictionary of the Words in the Greek Testament and The Hebrew Bible* (Bellingham, WA: Logos Bible Software, 2009), 20.

I spread out my hands to you;
  I thirst for you like a parched land.

Answer me quickly, Lord;
  my spirit fails.
Do not hide your face from me
  or I will be like those who go down to the pit.
Let the morning bring me word of your unfailing love,
  for I have put my trust in you.
Show me the way I should go,
  for to you I entrust my life.
Rescue me from my enemies, Lord,
  for I hide myself in you.
Teach me to do your will,
  for you are my God;
may your good Spirit
  lead me on level ground.

LINGER

Read the passage again out loud.

Are the same words or phrases you marked the first time still standing out?
Write them down. How do these words or phrases apply to your life right now?

LEARN

As you read the text for a third time, ask yourself, "How is God inviting me to
respond? What does He want me to be learning from this?" Write out what comes
to mind.

Read the passage one last time and answer these questions:

Why is God showing me this now?

What does this mean for my life?

What needs to change in my life?

How do I need to live differently?

PRAYER FOR THE DAY

Write a prayer below that "remembers the days of long ago." Write a prayer of gratitude for the many things God has done on your behalf.

TRUTH, LIES, AND ACTION

We've encountered a lot of introspective truths this week. Taking time to ground those truths and uproot the lies will bear fruit. So, it's that time again! Time for Truth, Lies, and Action:

TRUTH: A new way of looking at a truth from God's Word to replace the →
LIES: We want to name the lies we've believed and reclaim them with new truths to move us into →
ACTION: Because faith without works is dead (James 2:20), we want to be people of action. We will be looking today and tomorrow at specific action steps we can take to come out of hiding.

TRUTH: Our memory verses say: *God saved you by his grace when you believed. And you can't take credit for this; it is a gift from God. Salvation is not a reward for the good things we have done, so none of us can boast about it. For we are God's master-piece. He has created us anew in Christ Jesus, so we can do the good things he planned for us long ago. (Ephesians 2:8–10 NLT)*

TRUTH tells us we are loved and accepted by God because of His grace and rich mercy and not because of works, so we cannot possibly boast.

What other truths did you discover this week?

LIES: The LIE tells us many things. It tells us God can't possibly love us because of what we've thought, how we've felt, or what we've done. It tells us we are not accepted by God when we are, in fact, redeemed and belong to Him. It can also tell us we aren't hiding anything and deserve more than we are being given.

What other lies did you discover this week?

ACTION: Over the next few days, consider one of these action steps to help you take back the megaphone and come out of hiding:

- Find one trustworthy friend and share something you learned about yourself this week.
- Do you currently have a fear you need to surrender to Jesus? Write it down, share it with at least one other person, and ask that person to pray over you to be released from that fear.
- Take some time to make a list of 10–15 reasons you can absolutely trust God. Base your list on the ways He has been faithful in the past. Share your list with at least one other person, and explain why you chose each of those reasons.

Write about your ACTION step below. Share why you chose it and what the results were.

PRAYER FOR THE DAY

Lord Jesus, thank You for all the ways You show up over and over again. Give me the courage to speak truth to those around me. Give me the courage to be my true self—the person You have accepted and loved. Show me where I am hiding. Grab my hand and pull me out of the darkness and into the light. Amen.

you are

not alone

A person standing alone can be attacked and defeated, but two can stand back-to-back and conquer. Three are even better, for a triple-braided cord is not easily broken. **ECCLESIASTES 4:12 NLT**

Relationships are a beautiful mess at times. They can wound and they can heal, and sometimes one relationship can do both. I know I can be myself with my true spiritual friends and not have to hide. I can be a mess without anyone trying to fix me. I can share my ugliness and hear the truth in love. I can talk about how hard it is without feeling like a failure. I walk away from conversations with my spiritual friends knowing how much God loves me and desiring to be more like Jesus.

Throughout this week, we will work through Scriptures to enhance our relationships with others. Having spiritual friendships first requires *being* a spiritual friend. Understanding how God expects us to love and interact with each other is critical to this quest. We were created to connect, both with God and with others. This connection is hardwired into our very souls. Without connection, we wither and die. Pray this week for God to reveal those around you who are your connections. Give those relationships the care they need to grow into the beautiful, life-giving founts they were meant to be.

INTRODUCTION TO WEEK 4

WHY CHOOSE SPIRITUAL FRIENDSHIPS?

Fourth grade stunk. I was a misfit kind of kid. My friends and I had some sort of falling out, and I was shunned on the playground; my friends wouldn't talk to me. My memory has buried and long forgotten the reason why. What I haven't forgotten is feeling alone, wondering where I fit in.

That year, I was in Mr. Waggoner's class. He was a phenomenal teacher and made learning fun. He taught a crazy split classroom with third *and* fourth graders. Because of the crazy classroom deal, my cousin Brandi was in my class. When the shunning was going on and I didn't have anyone to play with, Brandi stayed with me. She made sure I wasn't alone.

My family has always been a place where I belong. We have the same noses, common taste buds, and a fierce and loyal love for one another. While I didn't feel like I fit anywhere at school in fourth grade, when I came home, I belonged. I know this is a gift not everyone experiences, unfortunately. Maybe your memories are flipped. Maybe you found a place at school to belong and at home you felt like a misfit. Maybe even now you are still searching for the place you belong and it pains you to know you haven't found it yet.

We all want to belong. At times, we wrestle with the deep desire to belong somewhere. We do what we can to fit in. We search for the places where we share common interests, passions, and loves.

God's original design for the church contains a built-in answer to this search for belonging. The church makes belonging possible. At times, we have missed the mark of God's original design, but there is much grace, and starting over is possible. Paul describes what it should look like in 1 Corinthians 12.

In verses 12–13, Paul says, "Just as a body, though one, has many parts, but all its many parts form one body, so it is with Christ. For we were all baptized by one Spirit so as to form one body—whether Jews or Gentiles, slave or free—and we were all given the one Spirit to drink." In other words, the body of the church is made up of smaller parts, but without each of those parts, the church is not whole. Our baptism in Christ is what gives us a place to belong. It doesn't matter what our history looks like; we have been made a part of the body of Christ.

Remember the cafeteria back in middle school? It's the age-old question: "Will there be a place for me at the table?" We want the invitation, but we fear it will never come. Paul tells us we have a place at the table. Jesus has invited us. We belong because He has made it so. We have been seated at the table with Jesus (Ephesians 2:6). The table is a growing table, too. There is always room for another chair.

Paul goes on to explain what it looks like to sit at this table. He explains how the body is not made up of one part but of many: hands and feet, eyes and ears, teeth, lips, fingers, toes, and knees. All of the parts have importance, purpose. At times, though, some parts begin thinking others have more value. Knees begin to think they do not belong because they are not an eye or a hand. But knees are important. Maybe they're not as glamorous as lips or fingernails, but they allow us to sit and bend down. Without them, walking would be difficult.

I'm not sure where you sit at the table or what is your part of the church body. I am sure of this: You have a purpose. Because this is true, you don't get to say you don't belong in the body of Christ. As a follower of Christ, He has given you a specific role the body needs you to fulfill so it can function properly. Paul asks, "If the whole body were an eye, where would the sense of hearing be? If the whole body were an ear, where would the sense of smell be?" (1 Corinthians 12:17). When we accept our place and choose to belong, everyone benefits.

God has placed each of us exactly where He wants us to be (verse 18). The original meaning of this phrase says God has appointed or deposited us where He desires or enjoys us to be. He delights in us flourishing and belonging. He loves to see us being and doing what He created us to be and do.

Sometimes I wrestle with believing I have a purpose. When others seem to have a grander invitation than I do, I think I am missing something and feel excluded. Just because I belong at God's table doesn't mean an invitation to *every* table is extended. Sometimes parts of the body take a rest.

The opposite can also be true. At times, I can begin to think I am more important than others because I get to do certain things. It's not a pretty part of my heart and is definitely something that will creep up at the most inopportune moments if it goes undetected. Paul has something to say about this. No part of the body gets to say to another, "I don't need you." Ever. In fact, those parts we deem less attractive or less critical are to be treated with special honor and elegance (verses 21–23). God has put the members of the body together. He has given greater honor to the parts lacking it (verse 24). Those parts had no nobility, but they received it from God. He bestowed honor on them.

You are no different. Jesus bestows honor on you, regardless of your place in the Kingdom. You are valuable. You are necessary, needed. You belong. You have a purpose and a place at the table. Others belong, too. They have a purpose and a place at the table. This truth is the beauty of the body of Christ.

We are connected. Just like our entire body feels infection or pain from another part; when one part of the body suffers, the entire part suffers with it. When one part is honored, every part should celebrate (1 Corinthians 12:26).

The yearning for belonging and connection is hardwired within us. Brené Brown, a researcher in social work, studied shame and vulnerability for over ten years. In her exploration, she discovered how our wiring for connection and belonging relates to shame and vulnerability. She spoke to people who were struggling to find connection and to those who were thriving.[17]

I find it remarkable that we are all hardwired for this connection and belonging. God created a place where we could find it. Not only did He say we belong to

17. Brené Brown's work on shame and vulnerability can be found in her book *Daring Greatly: How the Courage to Be Vulnerable Transforms the Way We Live, Love, Parent, and Lead* (New York: Gotham Books, 2012). She is also the author of *The Gifts of Imperfection: Let Go of Who You're Supposed to Be and Embrace Who You Are* (Hazelden, 2012) and *I Thought It Was Just Me (But It Isn't): Making the Journey from "What Will People Think?" to "I Am Enough"* (Gotham Books, 2007).

Him, but He gave us a group of people to walk with who are on the same journey. *We are not alone.* "There's something magical about the idea of twinkle lights shining in dark and difficult places," Brown says. "The lights are small, and a single light is not very special, but an entire strand of sparkling lights is sheer beauty. Connectivity makes them beautiful."[18] When we stand alone, the light we shine is minimal. Together, the light captivates, dances.

You may be thinking, "Well. That's great, but my experience hasn't been twinkle lights, especially in the church." We cannot always stand around holding hands and singing Michael W. Smith's "Friends Are Friends Forever." The truth is, sometimes, even when Jesus is the Lord of us, we aren't friends with some people forever. We experience seasons when friendships change and people grow apart. We also experience differing levels of connectivity with various people. God revealed this truth to me in a tough, but tangible way.

I was attending a conference workshop for songwriters. On the first day, I got to meet someone I had known of and admired, someone I wanted to talk shop with, someone who used generous words to describe other people's voices and songs. I longed to connect with her. But when I had a chance to ask her a question, she answered rather abruptly and moved away, doting on someone else. I got very little connection from her. It was a huge megaphone-in-the-wrong-hands moment for me. I was searching for belonging in a place I never should have been trying to find it. By the end of that day, my confidence was so low I concluded I should never try to write a song again and even doubted how I could have a place in the church at all (I told you it was a bad megaphone moment!).

The next morning, the rest of our team arrived at the workshop. I started explaining some of how I was feeling, and they were quick to combat the lies. That afternoon I strolled through the exhibit hall. A friend of mine told me about a woman I should meet who had a booth there. As I turned the corner, I saw this woman standing in front of a creative, artistic display. I introduced myself to her, and we talked for fifteen minutes without taking a breath. As I walked away, one of my team members knowingly said, "Seems like you connected with her."

18. Brené Brown, *Daring Greatly*, 40.

In that moment, God reminded me I will not connect with everyone at a deep level. I have my people, my tribe. I am called to love everyone, but I'm not called to connect with everyone at the same level. And neither are you.

To really connect, we must first learn what it means to be vulnerable. The word *vulnerability* carries baggage for many of us. So many people have stories of sharing themselves with someone else who handled their story poorly, wounding them severely. Vulnerability is defined as capable of being wounded or open to attack or damage; open to criticism or assault.[19] It seems safer to just stay hidden than to open ourselves to that kind of pain. We believe if we stay closed off from others, we somehow protect ourselves. We confuse vulnerability with weakness, which is defined as the inability to withstand attack or wounding.[20] Vulnerability cannot guarantee we will be safe, but it isn't weak. Vulnerability is courageous and brave. When we share our stories—the messy parts—with others, it is heroic. When we choose to protect ourselves, seeing vulnerability only as weakness, we rob ourselves of the connection we need.

So how do we know when to be vulnerable? We certainly don't want to walk around sharing everything with everybody. That's not what living in freedom looks like. Instead, we look for those deep connections. When we find people who can bear the weight of our story, we share it. I love the picture Brené Brown paints of those people. She describes choosing to be vulnerable with those who are on the ground in the arena fighting *with* you.[21]

You know who those people are. They're the ones who understand what you are fighting for. They know what the battle looks like. They defend you when you can't defend yourself. They aren't the people who are looking down from the stands making judgments about your situation, throwing the trash from their snacks at your feet. They are *with* you. They are *for* you. Just as we won't connect with everyone at the same level, we are not required to be vulnerable with everyone at the same level either.

19. Vulnerability. Dictionary.com. Dictionary.com Unabridged. Random House, Inc. http://dictionary.reference.com/browse/vulnerability.
20. Brené Brown, *Daring Greatly*, 39.
21. Ibid.

In Luke 5:17–26, we see a demonstration of these kinds of relationships. People all over the place were talking about how Jesus healed the sick. One day, Jesus was teaching to a large crowd. So many folks were crammed inside the house to hear Jesus that no one else could get close to Him. A group of guys had a paralyzed friend—and they wanted nothing more than to get him in front of Jesus. They wanted to change his story and see him healed, and they believed Jesus was the man who could do just that.

> These men carried their friend when he couldn't carry himself. *That* is what the body of Christ should look like.

Seeing the crowded mass of listeners blocking the door didn't dissuade them. They just found another way in. They climbed to the top of the house, dragging their friend with them. They were determined. They dug a hole and lowered him down from the roof, right in front of Jesus. Because of the faith of his friends, the paralyzed man's sins were forgiven, and he walked that day.

These men were in the arena with him. They carried him when he couldn't carry himself. They locked their shields with him, covering him when he couldn't fight. *That* is what the body of Christ should look like. You are not alone. We're in the arena fighting anyway, so let's just trade our fig leaves of shame for locked shields of faith. We'll all be better for it.

LINGER AND LEARN

Has your understanding of connection changed? In what way(s)?

Who are your connections? Where can you be vulnerable and be yourself?

How have you experienced the kind of "locked-shields" community the paralytic experienced in Luke 5? What does it take to cultivate that kind of community? How are you contributing?

Take a moment to thank God for the people in your life who allow you to be vulnerable.

TWO ARE BETTER THAN ONE

Sometimes I just like to do things alone. Because of what I do, most people find it hard to believe I'm an introvert. My work sometimes demands I possess extroverted tendencies, which can empty my tank. A common misunderstanding of the definition of introvert and extrovert has to do with whether or not a person loves people. In reality, it has more to do with where a person receives energy. I love people. I am relationally driven, but when I don't have some time alone to refuel, I drain quickly. Having time to myself is crucial for my sanity—and the sanity of those around me.

Being an introvert makes the text for today a little bit uncomfortable, but my guess is it might challenge you in a different way if you're an extrovert. Introverts have a tendency to "go it alone" at times, while extroverts might have a tendency to live at a surface level in their relationships. Because of their connection to and need for people, extroverts sometimes desire simply to keep others happy rather than go deep in a relationship.

Regardless of your introverted or extroverted nature, you were made to connect with others. God created you for relationships—yes, deep ones that allow you to be truly known by another person. This need for connection has many reasons, but I think one of the beautiful truths about how connection works for us is found in Ecclesiastes chapter 4.

Read slowly through Ecclesiastes 4:9–10, 12 in the New Living Translation:

> Two people are better off than one, for they can help each other succeed. If one person falls, the other can reach out and help. But someone who falls alone is in real trouble. A person standing alone can be attacked and defeated, but two can stand back-to-back and conquer. Three are even better, for a triple-braided cord is not easily broken.

How have you seen the truth of this Scripture in your own life both in negative and positive ways?

Read Ecclesiastes 4:9–10, 12 in The Message:

> It's better to have a partner than go it alone. Share the work, share the wealth.
> And if one falls down, the other helps, but if there's no one to help, tough! By yourself you're unprotected. With a friend you can face the worst. Can you round up a third? A three-stranded rope isn't easily snapped.

Describe a time when having someone walk alongside you in difficult circumstances kept you protected.

Why do you think this kind of community is important to God?

Think about a situation in your life when you felt alone and you wished you had someone walking with you. What was it like?

Who are your Ecclesiastes 4, "locked-shield" people? With whom do you feel protected?

Take a moment today to write one of those "locked-shields" friends a note of encouragement and thank them for walking with you through the difficult times.

Take a moment to write a prayer of gratitude for those people in your life who keep you from "going it alone." If you are in need of a group of people like this, write a prayer asking God to lead you to these friendships. He is faithful and will do it.

WEEK 4 | DAY 2

LIKE-MINDED LOVE

I've heard it said ministry in the church would be great if it weren't for the people. Sometimes we can have the same thoughts about relationships. The problem with relationships is they involve other people. The conflicts I have with myself are infrequent, and I would suppose you'd say the same. I typically don't disagree with myself. (It has happened on occasion, but rarely.)

Our flesh does not allow us to fall easily into relationships—especially deep ones. Those take a considerable amount of work. Not only does our flesh get in the way, but our fear and our pride also scream, "No! This is not the way I want to go!"

Jesus' ministry revolved around people. He spoke with the marginalized. He dined with the dirty. He healed the least of these. People and relationships mattered to Him. Since people and relationships mattered to Jesus, they should matter to us as well.

Humility is the key to any real relationship. If a person is coming to the relationship table expecting something all the time, it will run dry very quickly. Paul gives a beautiful recipe for humility in Philippians 2. He makes his case passionately:

> Therefore if you have any encouragement from being united with Christ, if any comfort from his love, if any common sharing in the Spirit, if any tenderness and compassion, then make my joy complete by being like-minded, having the same love, being one in spirit and of one mind. Do nothing out of selfish ambition or vain conceit. Rather, in humility value others above yourselves, not looking to your own interests but each of you to the interests of the others. (verses 1–4)

These verses seem to roll right off the tongue and solicit an "amen" from the crowd, but isn't this difficult? I'm constantly looking to my own interests, and I have to make a distinct effort to see the world from a different point of view than my own. My perspective is myopic. I have to think hard about understanding someone else's vantage point. I don't like this about myself, but my pride loves to lead my thoughts, words, and actions.

Paul goes on to write:

> In your relationships with one another, have the same mindset as Christ Jesus:
>
> Who, being in very nature God,
>   did not consider equality with God something to be used to his own advantage;
> rather, he made himself nothing
>   by taking the very nature of a servant,
>   being made in human likeness.
> And being found in appearance as a man,
>   he humbled himself
>   by becoming obedient to death—
>   even death on a cross!
>
> Therefore God exalted him to the highest place
>   and gave him the name that is above every name,
> that at the name of Jesus every knee should bow,
>   in heaven and on earth and under the earth,
> and every tongue acknowledge that Jesus Christ is Lord,
>   to the glory of God the Father. (verses 5–11)

"In your relationships with one another, have the same mindset as Christ Jesus." Again, easy to say, but complicated to carry out. Jesus was given a place of high honor for humbling Himself and being obedient to the Father.

Paul writes in verses 14–16:

> Do everything without grumbling or arguing, so that you may become blameless and pure, "children of God without fault in a warped and crooked generation." Then you will shine among them like stars in the sky as you hold firmly to the word of life. And then I will be able to boast on the day of Christ that I did not run or labor in vain.

Have you ever made it through an entire day without complaining, grumbling, or arguing? No? Well, me either. At least one thing in my life awakens grumbling or arguing each day. I'm not proud of this, and I know I do not want to continue down this path. I want to shine like stars. I would suspect people don't want to be around others who are grumbling and complaining all the time. I know I don't. I want to bring light and joy to those I'm around. More than anything, I want to be more like Jesus.

What this text isn't asking us to do is walk around being "happy." Shining like stars means we are carriers of the light of Christ. It's not a fake face we put on pretending everything is okay. The kind of grumbling and arguing Paul refers to seeks to tear down others. We are to build each other up, encourage and support, carry and champion. Typically when I'm complaining or grumbling or arguing, I'm looking to my own interests and not to the interests of others.

How does this text in Philippians relate to your spiritual friendships?

When have you thought of yourself "more highly than you ought" (Romans 12:3) in your friendships/core relationships? What effect did it have?

Think about a time when you didn't think of yourself "more highly than you ought" in a friendship or a core relationship. How did it affect the relationship?

Take a moment today to pray through this humility prayer attributed to St. Francis. Circle words or phrases that strike you. Ask God to make this prayer a true desire of your heart.

O Jesus, meek and humble of heart, hear me.
From the desire of being esteemed, deliver me, Jesus.
From the desire of being loved, deliver me, Jesus.
From the desire of being praised, deliver me, Jesus.
From the desire of being preferred to others, deliver me, Jesus.
From the desire of being consulted, deliver me, Jesus.
From the desire of being approved, deliver me, Jesus.
From the fear of being humiliated, deliver me, Jesus.
From the fear of being despised, deliver me, Jesus.
From the fear of being rebuked, deliver me, Jesus.
From the fear of being criticized, deliver me, Jesus.
From the fear of being forgotten, deliver me, Jesus.
From the fear of being ridiculed, deliver me, Jesus.
From the fear of being wronged, deliver me, Jesus.

From the fear of being suspected, deliver me, Jesus.

That others may be loved more than I, Jesus grant me the grace to desire it.

That others may be esteemed more than I, Jesus grant me the grace to desire it.

That in the opinion of the world others may increase and I may decrease, Jesus grant me the grace to desire it.

That others may be chosen and I set aside, Jesus grant me the grace to desire it.

—Francis of Assisi, Italian monk (1181–1226).[22]

22. Kurt Bjorklund, *Prayers for Today* (Chicago: Moody, 2011), 118.

CLOTHE YOURSELVES

Remember the nightmare about being naked in the middle of the junior high cafeteria with a crowd of laughing preteens pointing at you? We know we need to be clothed. We fear not being covered.

In the very first game of hide and seek, Adam and Eve made clothes out of fig leaves. In an effort to hide their nakedness, they sewed together an insufficient covering. God intervened and made them appropriate garments to withstand the weather and the tasks ahead of them. God covered their shameful nakedness, clothing them with what they need.

In the book of Colossians, Paul explains how a person who has been raised to new life in Christ and is a part of "God's chosen people, holy and dearly loved," should be clothed. He tells us what to "put to death," or take off, and remove from our lives.

> Put to death, therefore, whatever belongs to your earthly nature: sexual immorality, impurity, lust, evil desires and greed, which is idolatry. Because of these, the wrath of God is coming. You used to walk in these ways, in the life you once lived. But now you must also rid yourselves of all such things as these: anger, rage, malice, slander, and filthy language from your lips. (Colossians 3:5–8)

These things defile relationships. These things do not set you apart as a child of God, holy and dearly loved. This list brings shame that keeps us from emerging as ourselves. Paul goes on to say:

> Do not lie to each other, since you have taken off your old self with its practices and have put on the new self, which is being renewed in knowledge in the image of its Creator. Here there is no Gentile or

Jew, circumcised or uncircumcised, barbarian, Scythian, slave or free, but Christ is all, and is in all. (Colossians 3:9–11)

You are defined by Christ, regardless of your history or ethnicity or current standing with anyone. Jesus Christ gave His life to bring you a robe of righteousness, a garment of praise, a new covering you can exchange for your fig leaves.

With these observations in mind, read through Colossians 3:12–17 using the SOAP method of Bible study listed below. Let's begin!

S for Scripture:
Read slowly through the Scripture.

> Therefore, as God's chosen people, holy and dearly loved, clothe yourselves with compassion, kindness, humility, gentleness and patience. Bear with each other and forgive one another if any of you has a grievance against someone. Forgive as the Lord forgave you. And over all these virtues put on love, which binds them all together in perfect unity.
>
> Let the peace of Christ rule in your hearts, since as members of one body you were called to peace. And be thankful. Let the message of Christ dwell among you richly as you teach and admonish one another with all wisdom through psalms, hymns, and songs from the Spirit, singing to God with gratitude in your hearts. And whatever you do, whether in word or deed, do it all in the name of the Lord Jesus, giving thanks to God the Father through him.

O for Observations:
What are your observations about the text? What do you notice? What stands out? Underline those words or phrases. Write them below.

A for Application:

How is God calling you to apply the truth in this Scripture to your life right now? What is He calling you to change? How is He inviting you to be different?

P for Prayer:

What can you pray as a result of what God is calling you to do in this passage? What do you need to praise God for or request of Him in response? Write your prayer in the space below.

WE ARE EACH A PART

You and I are wired for connection. We want to belong, to feel needed, to be noticed. No one is exempt from this basic human need. First Corinthians 12:12–31 shares an interesting perspective on relationships within the church. You have a place. You belong. You are a part of something greater than yourself. You are wired for connection, and you have a place of belonging in the church. Today we are going to practice the SOAP method in this passage. Begin by reading the text below aloud slowly.

S for Scripture:
Read slowly through the Scripture.

> Just as a body, though one, has many parts, but all its many parts form one body, so it is with Christ. For we were all baptized by one Spirit so as to form one body—whether Jews or Gentiles, slave or free—and we were all given the one Spirit to drink. Even so the body is not made up of one part but of many.

> Now if the foot should say, "Because I am not a hand, I do not belong to the body," it would not for that reason stop being part of the body. And if the ear should say, "Because I am not an eye, I do not belong to the body," it would not for that reason stop being part of the body. If the whole body were an eye, where would the sense of hearing be? If the whole body were an ear, where would the sense of smell be? But in fact God has placed the parts in the body, every one of them, just as he wanted them to be. If they were all one part, where would the body be? As it is, there are many parts, but one body.

> The eye cannot say to the hand, "I don't need you!" And the head cannot say to the feet, "I don't need you!" On the contrary, those parts of the

body that seem to be weaker are indispensable, and the parts that we think are less honorable we treat with special honor. And the parts that are unpresentable are treated with special modesty, while our presentable parts need no special treatment. But God has put the body together, giving greater honor to the parts that lacked it, so that there should be no division in the body, but that its parts should have equal concern for each other. If one part suffers, every part suffers with it; if one part is honored, every part rejoices with it.

Now you are the body of Christ, and each one of you is a part of it. And God has placed in the church first of all apostles, second prophets, third teachers, then miracles, then gifts of healing, of helping, of guidance, and of different kinds of tongues. Are all apostles? Are all prophets? Are all teachers? Do all work miracles? Do all have gifts of healing? Do all speak in tongues? Do all interpret? Now eagerly desire the greater gifts.

O for Observations:

What are your observations about the text? What do you notice? What stands out? Mark the words or phrases in the text above.

A for Application:

How is God calling you to apply the truth in this Scripture to your life right now? What is He calling you to change? How is He inviting you to be different?

P for Prayer:

What can you pray as a result of what God is calling you to do in this passage? What do you need to praise God for or request of Him in response? Write your prayer in the space below:

LOVE ONE ANOTHER

We sat on the couch watching one of our family's favorite shows, *American Ninja Warrior*. Abigail's head was resting on my lap, and I was scratching her head. She paused and looked up at me and said in a sweet voice, "Mommy, I love you." My heart melted. She's a tough kid. She rarely shows her feelings outside of anger, and getting any sort of emotional response from her is sporadic at best. I treasured that moment.

Learning to love is difficult. Sometimes learning to express it is even harder. It's easier to love those who care for us and clearly have our best interests in mind. But loving those who do not is tricky business. Yet Jesus calls us to love one another. The only way this kind of love is possible is if we allow Jesus in us to do the loving. He is the source.

Today we will be engaging Scripture by listening, lingering, learning, then living. Read the passage four times with a different focus and set of questions each time.

Today's text is John 15:5–17.

LISTEN

Read the text printed for you below. Sit quietly for a moment before you begin. Ask the Holy Spirit to speak and show you what the Lord wants for you in this passage. Mark words or phrases that stand out as you read.

> I am the vine; you are the branches. If you remain in me and I in you, you will bear much fruit; apart from me you can do nothing. If you do not remain in me, you are like a branch that is thrown away and withers; such branches are picked up, thrown into the fire and burned. If you remain in me and my words remain in you, ask whatever you wish, and it will be done for you. This is to my Father's glory, that you bear much fruit, showing yourselves to be my disciples.

As the Father has loved me, so have I loved you. Now remain in my love. If you keep my commands, you will remain in my love, just as I have kept my Father's commands and remain in his love. I have told you this so that my joy may be in you and that your joy may be complete. My command is this: Love each other as I have loved you. Greater love has no one than this: to lay down one's life for one's friends. You are my friends if you do what I command. I no longer call you servants, because a servant does not know his master's business. Instead, I have called you friends, for everything that I learned from my Father I have made known to you. You did not choose me, but I chose you and appointed you so that you might go and bear fruit—fruit that will last—and so that whatever you ask in my name the Father will give you. This is my command: Love each other.

LINGER

Read the passage again out loud. Are the same words or phrases you marked the first time still standing out? Write them down. How do these words or phrases apply to your life right now?

LEARN

As you read the text for a third time, ask yourself, "How is God inviting me to respond? What does He want me to be learning from this?" Write out what comes to mind.

Read the passage one last time and answer these questions:

Why is God showing me this now?

What does this mean for my life?

What needs to change in my life?

How do I need to live differently?

Lord Jesus, thank You for being the source of love and for giving me an extra measure of Your grace so I can show it to others. Give me an extra ability to take Your love and give it to others. Show me when and where I'm not allowing You to love through me. Amen.

TRUTH, LIES, AND ACTION

Our relationships can carry the greatest potential for the megaphone to be in the wrong hands. We hurt people. People hurt us. We are all wounded and broken, and it shows. When discussing relationships and longing for deeper connections, deciphering the truth from the lies is important. So here we go! Time for Truth, Lies, and Action:

TRUTH: A new way of looking at a truth from God's Word to replace the →
LIES: We want to name the lies we've believed and reclaim them with new truths to move us into →
ACTION: Because faith without works is dead (James 2:20), we want to be people of action. We will be looking today and tomorrow at specific action steps we can take to come out of hiding.

TRUTH: Our memory verse says: *A person standing alone can be attacked and defeated, but two can stand back-to-back and conquer. Three are even better, for a triple-braided cord is not easily broken (Ecclesiastes 4:12 NLT).*

TRUTH tells us living in community is better than living alone. When we choose spiritual friendship, we are covered in the battle.

What other truths did you discover this week?

LIES: The LIE tells us many things. It tells us we are not worthy of deep relationship. It tells us we are not accepted by others and could not possibly bring anything of value to another person. It tells us we are too much of a mess for anyone to lock their shields with ours. These are all lies.

What other lies did you discover this week?

ACTION: Over the next few days, consider one of these action steps to help you take back the megaphone and come out of hiding:

- Find one trustworthy friend and share something you learned about yourself this week.
- Have you feared being vulnerable around a certain person? Is this person in the arena with you? If so, find a time to share a part of your story with her.
- What item from this week's study do you need to "put to death" or "put on"? Find a person you trust and share your list.
- Call or write a personal note to each person in your life who is allowing you to live without hiding. Send them a note of thanks for their incredible presence in your life.

Write about your ACTION step below. Share why you chose it and what the results were.

PRAYER FOR THE DAY

Lord Jesus, thank You for all the ways You continually show up in my life. Give me the courage to speak truth to those around me. Give me the courage to be my true self—the person You have accepted and loved—when I am around those who are on the ground fighting with me. Show me where I am hiding. Grab my hand and pull me out of the darkness and into the light. Amen.

you are

enough

MEMORY VERSES FOR WEEK 5:

For you died, and your life is now hidden with Christ in God. **COLOSSIANS 3:3**

Therefore, there is now no condemnation for those who are in Christ Jesus.
ROMANS 8:1

At this stage of the journey to freedom from hiding, we are looking at the truth of our identity and belonging. These Scriptures remind us we have been purchased with the life and blood of Jesus Christ. We have been clothed with righteousness and have been made into new creations with distinct purposes. Pray for God to solidify the truth of your relationship with Him this week. He loves you, He has redeemed you, and He is for you. Always.

INTRODUCTION TO WEEK 5

YOU DON'T HAVE TO HIDE ANYMORE

My grandmother made my dress for my senior recital in college. I remember picking out the silky, forest-green fabric and a beautiful, creamy lace she used to line the neck of the dress. She fashioned a drape that tied around my neck and flowed down the back. I had been outfitted for special occasions before, but this was a dress specially made with me in mind. I had never worn anything so special. As I sang my arias and art songs (poems set to music), I felt like a princess. With love, my grandmother carefully crafted the gown just for me.

I wonder if that's what Eve felt like in the garden. When God took her scrappy fig leaves and fitted garments for her from animal skin, I imagine she felt God's love for her. Perhaps she knew it was really grace covering her. Did she know an atonement had been made for the sin she committed? Did she understand that the shedding of blood was required for her to be whole again? She traded her shame for a new name.

God does the same with us. Isaiah 61 lays out the mission of Jesus through the Spirit of the Lord: "He has sent me to bind up the brokenhearted, to proclaim freedom for the captives and release from darkness for the prisoners . . . to comfort all who mourn . . ." He trades ashes for beauty, mourning for gladness, a spirit of despair for a garment of praise. He does all of this simply for the display of His splendor—for His glory alone (verses 1–3).

The Almighty God restores broken things. He trades the shattered heap for something exquisite. He says, "Instead of your shame, you will receive a double portion, and instead of disgrace you will rejoice in your inheritance . . . and everlasting joy will be yours" (verse 7). This exchange is not in God's favor, by any means.

Isaiah explains how his shame has been covered by God: "For he has clothed me with garments of salvation and arrayed me in a robe of his righteousness, as a bridegroom adorns his head like a priest, and as a bride adorns herself with her jewels" (verse 10).

> Redemption looks like a shattered pitcher becoming a brand-new, never-before-seen work of art.

These lavish garments are precious, one-of-a-kind coverings. They hold the same value as a bride's jewels. Isaiah 62 goes on to say, "You will be called by a new name that the mouth of the Lord will bestow" (verse 2). You will trade your shame for a new name because the Lord delights and rejoices in you (verse 4).

You have been made new. Jesus defeated sin and death so you could be a new creation. We are reconciled to God because God made Him who had no sin to be sin for us (2 Corinthians 5:14–21).

You are a *new* creation. What this means is you are *not* just a pitcher shattered into pieces and you've now been glued back together again. That's not a new creation. That's just a re-glued, broken-down pitcher. That kind of pitcher would have no purpose. Whatever liquid you put in it would leak out. The only thing it could do is sit on a shelf and remind everyone it was once broken. Redemption doesn't look like that.

Redemption looks like a shattered pitcher becoming a brand-new, never-before-seen work of art. Imagine God taking every single broken piece and constructing an intricate mosaic, where what once was the handle now serves as the sun in the upper corner. No one looks at the handle and thinks, "That handle isn't doing anyone any good." Sure, the artist knows what it once was and that it is no longer being used for that purpose, but everyone who lays eyes on the mosaic sees the sun and smiles.

Sometimes when we are the work of art, we are too close to see anything but the broken pieces. We remember how the handle was broken instead of looking at the whole picture and seeing the splendor God intended. New creations are perfect and intentional. Every piece is exactly where God purposefully placed it. His designs are flawless, and our re-creation is no different.

New creations are repurposed. When the pitcher breaks apart, it can no longer be useful for holding things. But when God makes it new, it will have a new purpose. The mosaic will be a thing of beauty doing what great art does: bringing joy, awe, and wonder to all who see it. When we are made new, we are given a new purpose in the kingdom. We're seated at the table and given something to do that brings value to everyone.

The most difficult aspect of new creations is that they take time. Instantaneous new creations are typically as good as microwaved food. I have a friend who smokes a lot of meat, and the meat he cooks is like nothing you've ever tasted before. It's amazing. I love to participate in eating the BBQ Brandon smokes, but I'm not patient enough to make it myself. But that's what makes it so good—time.

We like instant everything. Our own healing is no different. The best and lasting things take time. Most quick things are cheap substitutes. Being made new requires time to heal and time to grow. But just like the smoky BBQ, it's always worth the wait.

One benefit of being a new creation is a new hiding place. "For you died, and your life is now *hidden with Christ in God*" (Colossians 3:3).

When we choose Jesus, we get to hide in Him. He finds us and brings us out of darkness and into His wonderful light (1 Peter 2:9). We are fully known by Jesus and loved by Him. We've been raised with Christ, hidden with Him.

Romans 8:31–39 in The Message paints a picture of what it looks like to live in this new creation, hidden in a God who is for us:

So, what do you think? With God on our side like this, how can we lose? If God didn't hesitate to put everything on the line for us, embracing our condition and exposing himself to the worst by sending his own Son, is there anything else he wouldn't gladly and freely do for us? And who would dare tangle with God by messing with one of God's chosen? Who would dare even to point a finger? The One who died for us—who was raised to life for us!—is in the presence of God at this very moment sticking up for us. Do you think anyone is going to be able to drive a wedge between us and Christ's love for us? There is no way! Not trouble, not hard times, not hatred, not hunger, not homelessness, not bullying threats, not backstabbing, not even the worst sins listed in Scripture . . . None of this fazes us because Jesus loves us. I'm absolutely convinced that nothing—nothing living or dead, angelic or demonic, today or tomorrow, high or low, thinkable or unthinkable—absolutely nothing can get between us and God's love because of the way that Jesus our Master has embraced us.

Remember you are not what anyone else says you are. You are what God says you are:

God says you are His (Isaiah 43:1) and nothing can separate you from His love. (Romans 8:39)

You are not your past. You are not what you did. You are not what happened to you. You are an overcomer by the blood of the Lamb and the word of your testimony. (Revelation 12:11)

You are saved by grace. You are a masterpiece, created to do good works for Jesus. (Ephesians 2:8–10)

You are indeed a new creation—the old has gone and the new has come. (2 Corinthians 5:17)

Don't let anyone ever tell you otherwise.

Take a moment to read through Romans 8:31–39 again from The Message.

What has God repurposed in your life?

What have you seen God redeem and use for good in your life?

How have you been made new?

NEW GARMENTS

Comfy pants are beautiful. If there was a way I could somehow make a law requiring people to wear yoga pants on a regular basis, I would. The problem is, although a good pair of yoga pants is most definitely a gift from Jesus, they are not always appropriate to wear. Comfortable on my body, yes. Comfortable in every situation, no.

Unfortunately, I was created to be in situations where yoga pants just aren't the best choice. All of us are this way. You could certainly make a case that what you do 90 percent of the time could be done effectively in your comfy pants, but reality is 10 percent of the time you have to actually get dressed. In real clothes. But we like our comfy clothes. We like the way they move with us and don't remind us of the extra ice cream we ate last night.

Our comfy clothes are so much like the person we once were—the person we're trying to hide, the person who has been given a new wardrobe but still chooses to wear the old, worn, tattered yoga pants with a hole in the knee.

As daughters of the King, we've been invited to dance at the ball of the century—*just because we are His.* We've been given beautiful gowns, custom-fitted to our every curve, showing our most beautiful selves. Perhaps they aren't the most comfortable sometimes because they don't move with us exactly how we'd like them to, but in them, we are *stunning.*

Robes of righteousness are like this. They are like ball gowns, made especially for beautiful daughters of the King. Perfectly tailored to fit.

With these observations in mind, read through the following passage from Isaiah 61–62 using the SOAP method:

S for Scripture: Read slowly through the Scripture.

O for Observations: What are your observations about the text? What do you notice? What stands out?

A for Application: How is God calling you to apply the truth in this Scripture to your life right now? What is He calling you to change? How is He inviting you to be different?

P for Prayer: What can you pray as a result of what God is calling you to do in this passage? What do you need to praise God for or request of Him in response?

S for Scripture:
Read aloud slowly through the Scripture.

Today's Scripture reading contains two excerpts from Isaiah.

> The Spirit of the Sovereign Lord is on me,
>   because the Lord has anointed me
>   to proclaim good news to the poor.
> He has sent me to bind up the brokenhearted,
>   to proclaim freedom for the captives
>   and release from darkness for the prisoners,
> to proclaim the year of the Lord's favor
>   and the day of vengeance of our God,
> to comfort all who mourn,
>   and provide for those who grieve in Zion—
> to bestow on them a crown of beauty
>   instead of ashes,
> the oil of joy
>   instead of mourning,
> and a garment of praise
>   instead of a spirit of despair.

They will be called oaks of righteousness,
  a planting of the Lord
  for the display of his splendor.
  (Isaiah 61:1–3)

I delight greatly in the Lord;
  my soul rejoices in my God.
For he has clothed me with garments of salvation
  and arrayed me in a robe of his righteousness,
as a bridegroom adorns his head like a priest,
  and as a bride adorns herself with her jewels.
 For as the soil makes the sprout come up
  and a garden causes seeds to grow,
so the Sovereign Lord will make righteousness
  and praise spring up before all nations.

For Zion's sake I will not keep silent,
  for Jerusalem's sake I will not remain quiet,
till her vindication shines out like the dawn,
  her salvation like a blazing torch.
The nations will see your vindication,
  and all kings your glory;
you will be called by a new name
  that the mouth of the Lord will bestow.
You will be a crown of splendor in the Lord's hand,
  a royal diadem in the hand of your God.
No longer will they call you Deserted,
  or name your land Desolate.
But you will be called Hephzibah,
  and your land Beulah;
for the Lord will take delight in you,
  and your land will be married.
 As a young man marries a young woman,

so will your Builder marry you;
   as a bridegroom rejoices over his bride,
      so will your God rejoice over you.
   (Isaiah 61:10–62:5)

O for Observations:

What are your observations about the text? What do you notice? What stands out?

A for Application:

How is God calling you to apply the truth in this Scripture to your life right now? What is He calling you to change? How is He inviting you to be different?

P for Prayer:

What can you pray as a result of what God is calling you to do in this passage? What do you need to praise God for or request of Him in response? Write your prayer in the space below:

NOTHING CAN SEPARATE

I mess up a lot. Sometimes it's the same way over and over again, and sometimes it's a new kind of chaos, altogether different. I'm grateful there's not a punch card for the number of times you can mess up, or I'd be in a heap of trouble. Mine would have run out a long time ago.

If you are in Christ, you are forgiven. Period. You can't do anything to separate yourself from the love of Christ. Fully grasping this truth is difficult at times. Because we live in a merit-based society, everything is basically a barter, and people's approval of us wavers a great deal. We exchange everything. But with God, you are forgiven. Entirely. *Nothing* can separate you from the love of God in Christ Jesus.

With these observations in mind, read through the following passages from Romans 8 using the SOAP method listed below:

S for Scripture: Read slowly through the Scripture.

O for Observations: What are your observations about the text? What do you notice? What stands out?

A for Application: How is God calling you to apply the truth in this Scripture to your life right now? What is He calling you to change? How is He inviting you to be different?

P for Prayer: What can you pray as a result of what God is calling you to do in this passage? What do you need to praise God for or request of Him in response?

S for Scripture:
Read slowly through the Scripture. Underline words or phrases that stand out as you read. Take a moment to linger with the promises of Christ in this passage.

Therefore, there is now no condemnation for those who are in Christ Jesus, because through Christ Jesus the law of the Spirit who gives life has set you free from the law of sin and death. For what the law was powerless to do because it was weakened by the flesh, God did by sending his own Son in the likeness of sinful flesh to be a sin offering. And so he condemned sin in the flesh, in order that the righteous requirement of the law might be fully met in us, who do not live according to the flesh but according to the Spirit. (Romans 8:1–4)

Who shall separate us from the love of Christ? Shall trouble or hardship or persecution or famine or nakedness or danger or sword? As it is written:

"For your sake we face death all day long;
 we are considered as sheep to be slaughtered."
 No, in all these things we are more than conquerors through him who loved us. (Romans 8:35–37)

What, then, shall we say in response to these things? If God is for us, who can be against us? He who did not spare his own Son, but gave him up for us all—how will he not also, along with him, graciously give us all things? Who will bring any charge against those whom God has chosen? It is God who justifies. Who then is the one who condemns? No one. Christ Jesus who died—more than that, who was raised to life—is at the right hand of God and is also interceding for us. Who shall separate us from the love of Christ? Shall trouble or hardship or persecution or famine or nakedness or danger or sword? As it is written:

"For your sake we face death all day long;
 we are considered as sheep to be slaughtered."
 No, in all these things we are more than conquerors through him who loved us. For I am convinced that neither death nor life, neither angels nor demons, neither the present nor the future, nor any powers, neither

height nor depth, nor anything else in all creation, will be able to separate us from the love of God that is in Christ Jesus our Lord. (Romans 8:31–39)

O for Observations:

What are your observations about the text? What do you notice? What stands out?

A for Application:

How is God calling you to apply the truth in this Scripture to your life right now? What is He calling you to change? How is He inviting you to be different?

P for Prayer:

What can you pray as a result of what God is calling you to do in this passage? What do you need to praise God for or request of Him in response? Write your prayer in the space below:

NEW CREATION

Sometimes people tell me I'm creative. Most of the time, I don't feel that way. I think it's because I'm really more of an imitator. Even though I can think with originality at times, I am incapable of creating something out of nothing. I pretty much just innovatively organize. I can't create anything from dust, and there's a reason.

God is the Creator. He's not just a really creative person; He's THE Creator—the source of all created things. Because He is the Creator, He can repurpose and re-create anything He chooses. Just as He created Eve from Adam's rib—something repurposed—He is making each of us brand-new.

New creations are perfect. While they may look broken from some angles, they are made into exactly what God designs them to be.

New creations take time. Remember, instantaneous new creations are typically as good as microwaved food. Not so great when compared to a slowly cooked meal with time to marinate and simmer.

New creations are intentional. An artist typically has a vision in mind when beginning a new work. He or she may not have a complete picture, but likely has a directional, intentional vision. God *does* have the complete picture, though, and His work is completely accurate.

New creations are repurposed. When refurbished pieces are used in a new work, they are given life they did not have previously.

How have you seen God do these four things as He has made you new?

With these truths in mind, we will be encountering Scripture through our four-part process. We will listen, linger, learn, and then live. Let's dig in.

Read through the given passage four times. Four different sets of questions will help you encounter the text in a fresh, new way and hopefully bring life to your bones. Remember, it's not about simply completing the repetition. It's about lingering and listening to the Holy Spirit to see what needs to be learned and ultimately lived. We want to be changed by our time in God's Word.

Today's text is 2 Corinthians 5:11–21.

LISTEN

Read today's passages. Sit quietly for a moment before you begin. Ask the Holy Spirit to speak and show you what the Lord wants for you in this passage. Mark words or phrases that stand out as you read.

> Since, then, we know what it is to fear the Lord, we try to persuade others. What we are is plain to God, and I hope it is also plain to your conscience. We are not trying to commend ourselves to you again, but are giving you an opportunity to take pride in us, so that you can answer those who take pride in what is seen rather than in what is in the heart. If we are "out of our mind," as some say, it is for God; if we are in our right mind, it is for you. For Christ's love compels us, because we are convinced that one died for all, and therefore all died. And he died for all, that those who live should no longer live for themselves but for him who died for them and was raised again.
>
> So from now on we regard no one from a worldly point of view. Though we once regarded Christ in this way, we do so no longer. Therefore, if anyone is in Christ, the new creation has come: The old has gone, the new is here! All this is from God, who reconciled us to himself through Christ and gave us the ministry of reconciliation: that God was reconciling the world to himself in Christ, not counting people's sins

against them. And he has committed to us the message of reconciliation. We are therefore Christ's ambassadors, as though God were making his appeal through us. We implore you on Christ's behalf: Be reconciled to God. God made him who had no sin to be sin for us, so that in him we might become the righteousness of God.

LINGER

Read the passage again out loud. Are the same words or phrases you marked the first time still standing out? Write them down. How do these words or phrases apply to your life right now?

LEARN

As you read the text for a third time, ask yourself, "How is God inviting me to respond? What does He want me to be learning from this?" Write out what comes to mind.

LIVE

Read the passage one last time and answer these questions:

Why is God showing me this now?

What does this mean for my life?

What needs to change in my life?

How do I need to live differently?

Lord Jesus, thank You for making me new. You have not left me in the sin and shame of my past, but You have created something new in me. Help me to see the new creation You are making in me. Give me the patience I need to allow You to create in me what You desire. Help me to go willfully where You are leading me. Show me the new purpose You have given me. Thank You for all You are re-creating in me. Amen.

WEEK 5 | DAY 4

NEW NAMES

Throughout this journey, we have uncovered many truths. We have discovered the motivation of those involved in the very first game of hide and seek in Genesis 3 and how it affects us today. We know God is always for us, for man and for woman, and the enemy is looking to destroy us completely. Until the final battle between God and the enemy, we will have a struggle to keep the megaphone tightly gripped in our hands. The enemy will be consistently working to defeat us in whatever way he possibly can. His job is to take us out of the arena. Completely.

But that's not your story. Your story is a powerful one about how God has redeemed you, restored you, and made you into a new creation—a creation completely known and loved by God. A new creation with new purpose.

Over and over in the Bible, God grants new names as a part of restoration. When someone has a new purpose or calling, a new name is given. Just as He allowed Eve to be named after she sinned, God uses new names for redemptive reconciliation.

Abram was the first person to be renamed in the Bible. Prior to God's changing his name, Abram struggled. For example, God asked Abram to leave his father's household and his country—in other words, all that was familiar—to follow Him into a land He would later reveal. And Abram followed. Other times of trouble erupted with his nephew Lot; but God enabled Abram to keep peace with him and later allowed him to rescue Lot from captivity. And most incredibly, though Abram and his wife, Sarai, had long been childless, God promised Abram that he would be the father of many nations. God made a covenant with Abram that his offspring would be as numerous as the stars in the sky.

Yet even in the midst of the amazing relationship Abram had with God in which God showed His faithfulness, he struggled. He misled Pharaoh, neglecting to tell him Sarai was his wife (using a technicality to call her his sister), bringing disease on the Pharaoh's entire house as a result. Rather than waiting for God to fulfill His promise to make him a father of many nations, he married Sarai's maidservant Hagar in an attempt to fulfill God's blessing for a child on his own terms. You can read of these events in Genesis 12–16. Abram was ninety-nine years old when God gave him a new name.

Now let's pick up the narrative and read through Abram's story in Genesis 17:1–22.

What do you think it meant for Abram to receive a new name from God?

How did God show grace and compassion on both Abram and Sarai?

You, too, have been given a new name and have been repurposed for HIS kingdom.

Whoever has ears, let them hear what the Spirit says to the churches. To the one who is victorious, I will give some of the hidden manna. I will also give that person a white stone with a new name written on it, known only to the one who receives it. (Revelation 2:17)

Remember what God says about who you are.

How has God made you into a new creation? Take a moment to reflect on the transformation God has allowed in your life. How have you been made new?

What were the names you had previously? What does God call you now? What is your new name?

Lord Jesus, thank You for reminding me nothing is ever wasted. Thank You for giving me a new name and for making me an overcomer through You, through the story You have written on my heart. Help me to tell Your story through mine. Show me how to do this most effectively for Your kingdom. Amen.

REMEMBERING WHO YOU ARE

I have a terrible memory. I can remember details of projects I'm working on or things that are important right now, but I don't remember much about the past. My family would agree with me on this one. It has fueled their ability to make fun of me. A lot. I'm not exactly sure why I don't remember things well. It's kind of unfortunate in many instances.

Remembering is important to God. Throughout the Old Testament, He consistently told the Israelites to remember. He would have them set up memorial stones as reminders of what He had done so they could tell the stories to their children again and again (Joshua 3–4).

We tend to forget what we don't choose to remember. That sounds profound, I know. All right, maybe it's completely obvious, but what we do not purposefully remember gets lost—forgotten. God knew His people. He knew they would forget what He had done—what He had told them. And we are no different. When we do not deliberately take the time to remember, we will forget.

Over the course of the last weeks, we have encountered a great deal of truth. Taking intentional time to remember what God has taught us is vital to true life transformation. If we are going to live without hiding, we have to commit to remembering who we are in Christ.

Today we are going to take a look back at Week 2 Day 2 when we looked through what God says about who we really are. Take a moment to read each statement, then look back at what you wrote in response; and now write a response today.

I am a child of God.

He came into the very world he created, but the world didn't recognize him. He came to his own people, and even they rejected him. But to all who believed him and accepted him, he gave the right to become children of God. (John 1:10–12 NLT)

Your Thoughts Now: How has your understanding of this truth changed?

I have been bought with a price. I belong to God.

You do not belong to yourself, for God bought you with a high price. (Corinthians 6:19–20 NLT)

Do not be afraid, for I have ransomed you. I have called you by name; you are mine. For I am the Lord, your God, the Holy One of Israel, your Savior. Others were given in exchange for you. I traded their lives for yours because you are precious to me. You are honored, and I love you. (Isaiah 43:1, 3–4 NLT)

Your Thoughts Now: How has your understanding of this truth changed?

I have been adopted as God's child.

Long before he laid down earth's foundations, he had us in mind, had settled on us as the focus of his love, to be made whole and holy by his love. Long, long ago he decided to adopt us into his family through Jesus Christ. (What pleasure he took in planning this!) He wanted us to enter into the celebration of his lavish gift-giving by the hand of his beloved Son. (Ephesians 1:4–6 MSG)

Your Thoughts Now: How has your understanding of this truth changed?

I have been redeemed and forgiven of all my sins.

For he has rescued us from the kingdom of darkness and transferred us into the Kingdom of his dear Son, who purchased our freedom and forgave our sins. (Colossians 1:13–14 NLT)

Your Thoughts Now: How has your understanding of this truth changed?

I am complete in Christ.

For in Christ lives all the fullness of God in a human body. So you also are complete through your union with Christ, who is the head over every ruler and authority. For you were buried with Christ when you were baptized. And with him you were raised to new life because you trusted the mighty power of God, who raised Christ from the dead. (Colossians 2:9–10, 12 NLT)

Your Thoughts Now: How has your understanding of this truth changed?

I cannot be separated from the love of God.

> I am convinced that nothing can ever separate us from God's love. Neither death nor life, neither angels nor demons, neither our fears for today nor our worries about tomorrow—not even the powers of hell can separate us from God's love. No power in the sky above or in the earth below—indeed, nothing in all creation will ever be able to separate us from the love of God that is revealed in Christ Jesus our Lord. (Romans 8:38–39 NLT)

Your Thoughts Now: How has your understanding of this truth changed?

I have not been given a spirit of fear, but a spirit of power, love, and a sound mind.

> For God has not given us a spirit of fear and timidity, but of power, love, and self-discipline. So never be ashamed to tell others about our Lord. . . . With the strength God gives you, be ready to suffer with me for the sake of the Good News. (2 Timothy 1:7–8 NLT)

Your Thoughts Now: How has your understanding of this truth changed?

I am God's workmanship and am wonderfully made.

For we are God's masterpiece. He has created us anew in Christ Jesus, so we can do the good things he planned for us long ago. (Ephesians 2:10 NLT)

For you created my inmost being; you knit me together in my mother's womb. I praise you because I am fearfully and wonderfully made; your works are wonderful, I know that full well. My frame was not hidden from you when I was made in the secret place, when I was woven together in the depths of the earth. Your eyes saw my unformed body; all the days ordained for me were written in your book before one of them came to be. (Psalm 139:13–16)

Your Thoughts Now: How has your understanding of this truth changed?

I may approach God with freedom and confidence.

In him and through faith in him we may approach God with freedom and confidence. (Ephesians 3:12)

For we do not have a high priest who is unable to empathize with our weaknesses, but we have one who has been tempted in every way, just as we are—yet he did not sin. Let us then approach God's throne of grace with confidence, so that we may receive mercy and find grace to help us in our time of need. (Hebrews 4:15–16)

Your Thoughts Now: How has your understanding of this truth changed?

Choose the truth that is the most difficult for you to believe. Write a prayer asking God to help you believe this truth and live as though it were true.

TRUTH, LIES, AND ACTION

Trading lies for truth has proven essential in this battle with shame. Standing on the truth is the only solid way out of hiding. With that said, here it is! Time for Truth, Lies, and Action:

TRUTH: A new way of looking at a truth from God's Word to replace the →

LIES: We want to name the lies we've believed and reclaim them with new truths to move us into →

ACTION: Because faith without works is dead (James 2:20), we want to be people of action. We will be looking today and tomorrow at specific action steps we can take to come out of hiding.

Our memory verses for this week say:

For you died, and your life is now hidden with Christ in God. (Colossians 3:3)

Therefore, there is now no condemnation for those who are in Christ Jesus. (Romans 8:1)

TRUTH: TRUTH tells us we are not condemned if we are in Christ, regardless of our sin in the past. We are hidden with Christ and are safe. We have been made enough by the sacrifice of Jesus Christ on the cross.

What other truths did you discover this week?

LIES: The LIE tells us many things. It tells us we are not worthy of deep relationship. It tells us we are not accepted by others and could not possibly bring anything of value to another person. It tells us we are too much of a mess for anyone to lock their shields with ours. These are all lies.

What other lies did you discover this week?

ACTION: Over the next few days, consider one of these action steps to help you take back the megaphone and come out of hiding:

- Find one trustworthy friend and share something you learned about yourself this week.
- Are you still condemning yourself for something Christ has already forgiven? Take some time to sit before Jesus and allow Him to speak through the Holy Spirit the truth that you are forgiven and clean. Find someone to share this experience with who can remind you often you are indeed clean.
- Are you harboring resentment or a lack of forgiveness for someone who has also been made clean in Christ? Spend some time asking Jesus through His Holy Spirit to help you to release that bitter root. If you feel led to let the person know you have forgiven them, do so. Remind them of God's love for them.
- Take some time to write out your new purpose as a new creation and place it somewhere you can see it. If you'd rather get messy, find a pitcher or bowl you can break and glue into a mosaic to remind you of the beautiful purpose given to you as a masterpiece, re-created in Christ.

Write about your ACTION step below. Share why you chose it and what the results were.

PRAYER FOR THE DAY

Lord Jesus, You have made me beautiful. You have made me clean. You have made me whole. You have given me a purpose. You have made me enough. Because what You did on the cross—the life You gave for me—was enough to cover my shame. How could I ever need anything more than what You already gave? Help me to remember You gave everything You could and it indeed is enough. Remind me often. You are amazing. Amen.

you are

found:
the relentless pursuit of God

"My son," the father said, "you are always with me, and everything I have is yours. But we had to celebrate and be glad, because this brother of yours was dead and is alive again; he was lost and is found." **LUKE 15:31–32**

You are valuable to God the Father. He will search for you for as long as it takes. Even when you hide, He comes after you. He won't stop until you are found.

As we enter into our final stretch of the study, I am praying the truth you encounter this week will transform you—your view of God the Father, your understanding of His relentless and fierce love for you. I am praying you will know and experience the truth that indeed *you are found*.

THE RELENTLESS PURSUIT OF GOD

I grew up in the church and was baptized when I was eight years old. I remember being in high school and thinking that I didn't have a very dramatic conversion story. It seemed pretty uneventful really. I hadn't known what it meant to be "lost." Then I went to college.

I didn't make the best choices my freshman year of college. The faith I had carried through my youth couldn't carry me. I knew all of the right answers, but I didn't really know Jesus. I knew what it meant to sin and that I should try not to, but I didn't fully understand what a complete sinner I was. I had grown up with a list of the things you did or didn't do if you were a Christian. That list ruled my life instead of a relationship with Jesus.

One day I was sitting in my dorm room toward the end of my freshman year feeling alone, never having felt so empty. With the choices I had made weighing me down, I wrote a simple poem called "There's a Hole in My Heart." I have no idea where the poem is now, but I can remember exactly how I felt as I penned it.

Isolated. Hollow. Lost.

And oh, how I longed to be found. To be known. To be forgiven and clean. To have value because I was seen by the Creator and not because of what I did or didn't do. I missed Jesus. That vacant, hollow place in my soul, that hole in my heart, ached for His presence. I wept and begged Jesus to find me again. To show me how to live with Him now.

What I discovered is that while I walked away from Jesus, He never stopped pursuing me. He came after me with the full weight of His love the entire time. He never relented. Even when I didn't acknowledge Him, He tracked me down.

It's taken me many years to understand that conversion is a process. God has been writing my story since I took my first breath and will continue writing it until I take my last. Every time I have a new realization that leads to life transformation, I'm like a new convert. He beckons me to a deeper place of relationship with Him.

The value of lost and hiding things proves great with the Father. Every one of us holds significant value to God the Father. Jesus told three parables to the Pharisees who had great trouble comprehending that truth. The Pharisees were the ones who had the list of what to do down cold. In their severe practice of the law, they believed they earned God's favor. They assumed they had value to the Father *because* of their good deeds and perfect following of God's laws. As a result of that assumption, they also believed others who didn't follow the law couldn't possibly have value in the sight of God the Father.

So, Jesus schooled the Pharisees.

They had just been carping about how Jesus welcomed sinners and would even eat with them. Their judgment was brutal—both of Jesus and of the people He invited to be around Him. In the midst of their grousing, He told them a series of three related stories we find in Luke 15.

In the first story, Jesus talked about a shepherd who had a hundred sheep and lost just one. He relays how the shepherd wouldn't sleep until the one lost sheep was found. The shepherd left the ninety-nine sheep that were not lost to go on a hunt to find the one. Then Jesus explains how the shepherd responds when that one lost sheep is found—he picks up the sheep and joyfully carries it home on his shoulders. Then he calls his friends and neighbors to rejoice with him. He is so thrilled he has found the lost sheep that he can't keep the news to himself. It's just not possible.

In the second story, Jesus tells of a woman who owns ten silver coins and loses one. She doesn't rest until she finds it. She sweeps the house, searching everywhere until it is found. When she finally finds it, she responds the same way as the shepherd. She calls her friends and neighbors to rejoice with her.

In the third story, Jesus recounts a remarkable story of a father and his two boys. The younger son makes an intriguing request of his father, asking for his share of the estate. When the younger son receives his inheritance, he immediately goes on a little trip spending what he has, living it up, and squandering his money. I'm sure he had a blast while the cash flowed. Then famine happened, and he suddenly had nothing. He was in such need that he searched for work as a hired farmhand. He was so hungry that all he wanted to eat was the pig slop, but not even that was made available to him.

The text says, "When he came to his senses, he said, 'How many of my father's hired men have food to spare, and here I am starving to death! I will set out and go back to my father and say to him: Father, I have sinned against heaven and against you. I am no longer worthy to be called your son; make me like one of your hired servants'" (Luke 15:17–19). *When he came to his senses.* When he realized who he was didn't match his current situation, something happened in him. He recognized his need to go back to his father and confess his wrongdoing. He hoped there would be a place for him among the workers. The younger son was not asking for complete restoration. He just wanted to be fed and forgiven. Even in that hope, it was possible that his father would reject him and send him away. But he mustered the courage and set out for home.

And then the unexpected happened. Before he was even close, his father knew the approaching figure in the distance was him. His father lost himself in the joy of his son returning. "He ran to his son, threw his arms around him, and kissed him" (Luke 15:20). The younger boy squeaked out his rehearsed confession, "Father, I have sinned against heaven and against you. I am no longer worthy to be called your son."

And before the son could even get the last word out, the father is making plans for the feast that's coming. He cannot help it. He orders the best robe for him along with his own ring, and some sandals for his dusty feet. Not only does he give generously to his boy, but he orders the fattened calf butchered so they can have a party to celebrate his homecoming. Why all of this hoopla? Simple. His son was dead and is now alive. He was lost and now is found.

You see, each story Jesus told ended with the rejoicing that breaks out in heaven when someone who is lost is found. The party is grand. I imagine it's a feast like no other. There's a lot of high-fiving, fist-bumping, and jumping about.

There is nothing the Father loves more than when we are found.

> The very same is true for you. You have the same value as the lost sheep, lost coin, and lost son to God the Father. He rejoices when you come home. And He doesn't stop looking until you are found.

But the third story doesn't end there. We're reminded there was another character. Remember? The father had *two* sons. The older brother received his inheritance too. Filled with faithful responsibility, he stayed around to help his dad. He was dutiful, *righteous*.

When all of the hullabaloo and hype happens over his younger brother, he loses it. His anger keeps him from attending the party. In fact, he flat out refuses. His father begs him to join the festivities. He responds by listing all of the ways he's been a faithful son. Then he throws a bit of a toddler tantrum saying, "You never gave me even a young goat so I could celebrate with my friends. But when this son of yours who has squandered your property with prostitutes comes home, you kill the fattened calf for him!" (Luke 15:29–30). In other words, *how dare you!*

The father's words to him are not harsh. He simply says, "My son, you are always with me, and everything I have is yours. But we had to celebrate and be glad, because this brother of yours was dead and is alive again; he was lost and is found" (Luke 15:31–32). *You are always with me.* You are with me even when you don't recognize my presence with you. If you would have asked me for anything, I would have freely given it. I have seen your faithfulness. I celebrate you too. In the previous two stories, the focus is on what is lost. This third story has that element as well, but this additional character is a great illustration of the importance of remembering that we were all lost. Every single one of us was once without hope and God in the world, and it would do us good to remember that fact (Ephesians 2:12). How easily we can hold the older brother's attitude.

I've spent my fair share of time as a judgment-wielding Pharisee. It's not pretty and I'm not proud of it, but when I forget that my story is bruised and broken, it's easy to do.

I'm learning what it's like to accept my place as the younger brother, the lost sheep, the lost coin. It's difficult at times to believe God the Father sees my life as *that* valuable—valuable enough to leave the rest and come to drag me out of hiding to be found. Sometimes I lose my way and every time, there He is fiercely loving and pursuing me, and rejoicing when I come home.

The very same is true for you. You have the same value as the lost sheep, lost coin, and lost son to God the Father. He rejoices when you come home. And He doesn't stop looking until you are found.

LINGER AND LEARN

Take a moment to read Luke 15:11–32.

Which brother can you relate to the most? Why?

How do you feel knowing God the Father will not stop looking for you until you are found?

Take a moment to write down your own conversion story. When have you felt lost in your life? When did you find Jesus? What was that like?

WEEK 6 | DAY 1

LOST AND HIDDEN THINGS

It's possible this week's texts are familiar to you. They may not be and that's fine, but if they are, my prayer for you is that you will see something fresh and new in reading them along with the truths you have already encountered in mind. Today and tomorrow, we will spend time lingering in the three parables found in Luke 15, listening for what the Holy Spirit has to show us in the similar stories Jesus told.

Today we will interact with Scripture through our four-part process of listen, linger, learn, and then live. I'm trusting God to show you something remarkable today. Let's dig in!

Read through the given passage four times. Four different sets of questions will help you approach the text in a fresh, new way and hopefully bring life to your bones. It's not about simply completing the repetition. It's about lingering and listening to see what needs to be learned and ultimately lived. We want to be changed by our time in God's Word.

LISTEN

Read Luke 15 in your own Bible. Sit quietly for a moment before you begin. Ask the Holy Spirit to speak and show you what the Lord wants for you in this passage. Notice which words or phrases stand out as you read. Mark them and write them down.

LINGER

Read the passage again out loud. Are the same words or phrases you marked the first time still standing out? Write down the ones that are still lingering. How do these words or phrases apply to your life right now?

LEARN

As you read the text for a third time, ask yourself, "How is God inviting me to respond?"

What does He want me to be learning from this?

What are the common threads in the stories Jesus told?

What is the Holy Spirit saying in those threads to me? Write out what comes to mind.

LIVE

Read the passage one last time and answer these questions:

Why is God showing me this now?

What does this mean for my life?

What needs to change in my life?

How do I need to live differently?

PRAYER FOR THE DAY

Father God, thank You for giving me, a sinner, such great value in Your kingdom. Thank You for not leaving me behind. Ever. You have pursued me when I've been far from You and when I've been close. Thank You for Your unconditional pursuit of my heart and all its shattered pieces. You are an amazing God and I praise Your name. Amen.

THE SEARCH FOR SINNERS

Hebrews 4:12 says, "the word of God is alive and active." I love that we can read a passage from the Bible over and over again and God will show us a new layer of truth in it. The Word of God will not grow stale.

Sometimes when I repeat a reading, I forget this truth. I am trusting God to show you something more than what He showed you yesterday in your reading of the parables in Luke 15. Just like the sinners the Pharisees accused Jesus of loving and accepting by dining with them, Jesus invites us into the stories He tells. These words are for us. The invitation to be found comes from Christ Himself to each of us.

With this in mind, use the SOAP method to encounter the parables in Luke 15. Imagine yourself in the stories as you read. Picture Jesus telling you the stories.

S for Scripture:
Read aloud slowly through Luke 15 below in The Message.

> By this time a lot of men and women of doubtful reputation were hanging around Jesus, listening intently. The Pharisees and religion scholars were not pleased, not at all pleased. They growled, "He takes in sinners and eats meals with them, treating them like old friends." Their grumbling triggered this story.

> "Suppose one of you had a hundred sheep and lost one. Wouldn't you leave the ninety-nine in the wilderness and go after the lost one until you found it? When found, you can be sure you would put it across your shoulders, rejoicing, and when you got home call in your friends and neighbors, saying, 'Celebrate with me! I've found my lost sheep!' Count on it—there's more joy in heaven over one sinner's rescued life than over ninety-nine good people in no need of rescue.

"Or imagine a woman who has ten coins and loses one. Won't she light a lamp and scour the house, looking in every nook and cranny until she finds it? And when she finds it you can be sure she'll call her friends and neighbors: 'Celebrate with me! I found my lost coin!' Count on it—that's the kind of party God's angels throw every time one lost soul turns to God."

Then he said, "There was once a man who had two sons. The younger said to his father, 'Father, I want right now what's coming to me.'

"So the father divided the property between them. It wasn't long before the younger son packed his bags and left for a distant country. There, undisciplined and dissipated, he wasted everything he had. After he had gone through all his money, there was a bad famine all through that country and he began to hurt. He signed on with a citizen there who assigned him to his fields to slop the pigs. He was so hungry he would have eaten the corncobs in the pig slop, but no one would give him any.

"That brought him to his senses. He said, 'All those farmhands working for my father sit down to three meals a day, and here I am starving to death. I'm going back to my father. I'll say to him, Father, I've sinned against God, I've sinned before you; I don't deserve to be called your son. Take me on as a hired hand.' He got right up and went home to his father.

"When he was still a long way off, his father saw him. His heart pounding, he ran out, embraced him, and kissed him. The son started his speech: 'Father, I've sinned against God, I've sinned before you; I don't deserve to be called your son ever again.'

"But the father wasn't listening. He was calling to the servants, 'Quick. Bring a clean set of clothes and dress him. Put the family ring on his finger and sandals on his feet. Then get a grain-fed heifer and roast it. We're going to feast! We're going to have a wonderful time! My son is here—given up for dead and now alive! Given up for lost and now found!' And they began to have a wonderful time.

"All this time his older son was out in the field. When the day's work was done he came in. As he approached the house, he heard the music and dancing. Calling over one of the houseboys, he asked what was going on. He told him, 'Your brother came home. Your father has ordered a feast—barbecued beef!—because he has him home safe and sound.'

"The older brother stalked off in an angry sulk and refused to join in. His father came out and tried to talk to him, but he wouldn't listen. The son said, 'Look how many years I've stayed here serving you, never giving you one moment of grief, but have you ever thrown a party for me and my friends? Then this son of yours who has thrown away your money on whores shows up and you go all out with a feast!'

"His father said, 'Son, you don't understand. You're with me all the time, and everything that is mine is yours—but this is a wonderful time, and we had to celebrate. This brother of yours was dead, and he's alive! He was lost, and he's found!'"

O for Observations:

What are your observations about the text? What do you notice? What stands out?

A for Application:

As you imagine yourself in the story, how is God calling you to apply the truth in this Scripture to your life right now? What is He calling you to change? How is He inviting you to be different?

P for Prayer:

What can you pray as a result of what God is calling you to do in this passage? What do you need to praise God for or request of Him in response? Write your prayer in the space below:

THERE ALL ALONG

I can remember the one time I was ever called to the principal's office in school. I was a senior in high school and had brought a water bottle to class. What a rebel! No, I was actually the dutiful, responsible child. I made sure I did the right things even when I didn't want to. I didn't like to be in trouble. I also believed my success in doing the right things earned me acceptance and favor from others. That's really why I did the right things.

With that kind of background, I feel a connection with the older brother in the parable of the lost son. I'm not proud of it, but sometimes I can relate to the Pharisees. The unending grace of God doesn't always make sense.

I find it interesting that Jesus included the older brother in this story. He didn't have to do that, but He did.

As you read through Luke 15:11–32, think about the older brother. What can you learn from his response?

What is God inviting you to see in yourself through the older brother's perspective?

LISTEN

Read Luke 15:11–32 in a different version. It's printed for you in The Voice[23] paraphrase; you might also want to look it up in the English Standard Version or the New American Standard Bible (easily found at Biblegateway.com). Sit quietly

23. The Voice Bible Copyright © 2012 Thomas Nelson, Inc. The Voice™ translation © 2012 Ecclesia Bible Society All rights reserved.

for a moment before you begin. Ask the Holy Spirit to speak and show you what the Lord wants for you in this passage. Mark words or phrases that stand out as you read.

Once there was this man who had two sons. One day the younger son came to his father and said, "Father, eventually I'm going to inherit my share of your estate. Rather than waiting until you die, I want you to give me my share now." And so the father liquidated assets and divided them. A few days passed and this younger son gathered all his wealth and set off on a journey to a distant land. Once there he wasted everything he owned on wild living. He was broke, a terrible famine struck that land, and he felt desperately hungry and in need. He got a job with one of the locals, who sent him into the fields to feed the pigs. The young man felt so miserably hungry that he wished he could eat the slop the pigs were eating. Nobody gave him anything.

So he had this moment of self-reflection: "*What am I doing here*? Back home, my father's hired servants have plenty of food. Why am I here starving to death? I'll get up and return to my father, and I'll say, 'Father, I have done wrong—wrong against God and against you. I have forfeited any right to be treated like your son, but I'm wondering if you'd treat me as one of your hired servants?'" So he got up and returned to his father. The father looked off in the distance and saw the young man returning. He felt compassion for his son and ran out to him, enfolded him in an embrace, and kissed him.

The son said, "Father, I have done a terrible wrong in God's sight and in your sight too. I have forfeited any right to be treated as your son."

But the father turned to his servants and said, "Quick! Bring the best robe we have and put it on him. Put a ring on his finger and shoes on his feet. Go get the fattest calf and butcher it. Let's have a feast and celebrate because my son was dead and is alive again. He was lost and has been found." So they had this huge party.

Now the man's older son was still out in the fields working. He came home at the end of the day and heard music and dancing. He called one of the servants and asked what was going on. The servant said, "Your brother has returned, and your father has butchered the fattest calf to celebrate his safe return."

The older brother got really angry and refused to come inside, so his father came out and pleaded with him to join the celebration. But he argued back, "Listen, all these years I've worked hard for you. I've never disobeyed one of your orders. But how many times have you even given me a little goat to roast for a party with my friends? Not once! *This is not fair!* So this son of yours comes, this wasteful delinquent who has spent your hard-earned wealth on loose women, and what do you do? You butcher the fattest calf from our herd!"

The father replied, "My son, you are always with me, and all I have is yours. Isn't it right to join in the celebration and be happy? This is your brother we're talking about. He was dead and is alive again; he was lost and is found again!"

LINGER

Read the passage again out loud. Are the same words or phrases you marked the first time still standing out? Write them down. How do these words or phrases apply to your life right now?

LEARN

As you read the text for a third time, ask yourself, "How is God inviting me to respond? What does He want me to be learning from this?" Write out what comes to mind.

Read the passage one last time and answer these questions:

Why is God showing me this now?

What does this mean for my life?

What needs to change in my life?

How do I need to live differently?

PRAYER FOR THE DAY

Jesus, thank You for Your presence. Thank You for always being available to meet with me even when I don't choose to notice You. Help me to recognize all You've made available to me as Your child. Help me to remember that You value and love me whether I do the right thing or not. You cannot possibly love me any more or any less because of what I do or do not do. Thank You for Your unconditional grace, mercy, and love. Amen.

YOU ARE FOUND

It's taken a long time for me to fully embrace that I am a prodigal daughter. It might be because it's easier that way. It may be because I don't have a flashy testimony of deliverance. But in reality, I am. I am that child. The one who went her own way. The one who did what she wanted to do without regard for the Father. When I understand it in that way, I am astounded by the grace Jesus has lavished on me.

You are no different. Whether you have a dramatic story or not, Jesus views you as the prodigal child. His response to your return doesn't differ from the Father's response in the story.

Imagine yourself in the story as you read. You are the prodigal son. You are the one who has chosen to go out on your own. Imagine the Father is speaking to you.

LISTEN

Read Luke 15:11–32 in the New Living Translation. Sit quietly for a moment before you begin. Ask the Holy Spirit to speak, to show you what the Lord wants for you in this passage and to help you imagine yourself in the story. Mark words or phrases that stand out as you read.

> To illustrate the point further, Jesus told them this story: "A man had two sons. The younger son told his father, 'I want my share of your estate now before you die.' So his father agreed to divide his wealth between his sons.
>
> "A few days later this younger son packed all his belongings and moved to a distant land, and there he wasted all his money in wild living. About the time his money ran out, a great famine swept over the land, and he began to starve. He persuaded a local farmer to hire him, and the

man sent him into his fields to feed the pigs. The young man became so hungry that even the pods he was feeding the pigs looked good to him. But no one gave him anything.

"When he finally came to his senses, he said to himself, 'At home even the hired servants have food enough to spare, and here I am dying of hunger! I will go home to my father and say, "Father, I have sinned against both heaven and you, and I am no longer worthy of being called your son. Please take me on as a hired servant."'

"So he returned home to his father. And while he was still a long way off, his father saw him coming. Filled with love and compassion, he ran to his son, embraced him, and kissed him. His son said to him, 'Father, I have sinned against both heaven and you, and I am no longer worthy of being called your son.'

"But his father said to the servants, 'Quick! Bring the finest robe in the house and put it on him. Get a ring for his finger and sandals for his feet. And kill the calf we have been fattening. We must celebrate with a feast, for this son of mine was dead and has now returned to life. He was lost, but now he is found.' So the party began.

"Meanwhile, the older son was in the fields working. When he returned home, he heard music and dancing in the house, and he asked one of the servants what was going on. 'Your brother is back,' he was told, 'and your father has killed the fattened calf. We are celebrating because of his safe return.'

"The older brother was angry and wouldn't go in. His father came out and begged him, but he replied, 'All these years I've slaved for you and never once refused to do a single thing you told me to. And in all that time you never gave me even one young goat for a feast with my friends. Yet when this son of yours comes back after squandering your money on prostitutes, you celebrate by killing the fattened calf!'

"His father said to him, 'Look, dear son, you have always stayed by me, and everything I have is yours. We had to celebrate this happy day. For your brother was dead and has come back to life! He was lost, but now he is found!'"

LINGER

Read the passage again out loud. Are the same words or phrases you marked the first time still standing out? Write them down. How do these words or phrases apply to your life right now?

LEARN

As you read the text for a third time, ask yourself, "How is God inviting me to respond? What does He want me to be learning from this?" Write out what comes to mind.

LIVE

Read the passage one last time and answer these questions:

Why is God showing me this now?

What does this mean for my life?

What needs to change in my life?

How do I need to live differently?

Write a prayer of gratitude to the Father for His relentless pursuit of you.

WEEK 6 | DAY 5

LIVING NEW TRUTHS

Over the last six weeks, we have encountered many new truths to replace some of the lies the "megaphone" spouts when it is in the wrong hands. Remembering what God has said completely is an important practice to help to replace the lies with lasting new truths. The enemy will constantly use the "Did God *really* say?" line as many times as he possibly can. He is not very creative! When he begins with that line, remind him God DID really say all of this about you:

You are loved. (Isaiah 43:4)

You are beautiful. (Psalm 139:13–16)

You are created for a purpose. (Jeremiah 29:11)

You are enough. (Hebrews10:14)

You are found. (Luke 15:32)

Spend some time today going through the previous weeks of this study. The memory verses for each week are written below. Write down your insights from each week's lessons and the new truths God revealed to you. Write them in a prominent place—especially if you are having trouble believing they are true. I've heard it said the definition of believing is that we would live as though it were true. We want to live as though what we believe is really true. Take some time to linger in the lessons you've learned. Ask God to solidify new truths so you will believe them and live like you know they are true.

Week One—Fig Leaves Don't Hide Anything: Why Do We Hide?
Those who look to him are radiant; their faces are never covered with shame. (Psalm 34:5)

What new truths did you learn in Week One?

Week Two—Know Your Enemy: How Can We Win the War on Shame?

But now, this is what the LORD says—he who created you, Jacob, he who formed you, Israel: "Do not fear, for I have redeemed you; I have summoned you by name; you are mine." (Isaiah 43:1)

Be alert and of sober mind. Your enemy the devil prowls around like a roaring lion looking for someone to devour. (1 Peter 5:8)

What new truths did you learn in Week Two?

Week Three—Come Out, Come Out, Wherever You Are: Why Do We Really Hide?

God saved you by his grace when you believed. And you can't take credit for this; it is a gift from God. Salvation is not a reward for the good things we have done, so none of us can boast about it. For we are God's masterpiece. He has created us anew in Christ Jesus, so we can do the good things he planned for us long ago. (Ephesians 2:8–10 NLT)

What new truths did you learn in Week Three?

Week Four—You Are Not Alone: Why Choose Spiritual Friendships?

A person standing alone can be attacked and defeated, but two can stand back-to-back and conquer. Three are even better, for a triple-braided cord is not easily broken. (Ecclesiastes 4:12 NLT)

What new truths did you learn in Week Four?

Week Five—You Are Enough: You Don't Have to Hide Anymore

For you died, and your life is now hidden with Christ in God. (Colossians 3:3)
Therefore, there is now no condemnation for those who are in Christ Jesus. (Romans 8:1)

What new truths did you learn in Week Five?

Week Six—You Are Found: The Relentless Pursuit of God

"'My son,' the father said, 'you are always with me, and everything I have is yours. But we had to celebrate and be glad, because this brother of yours was dead and is alive again; he was lost and is found.'" (Luke 15:31–32)

What new truths did you learn in Week Six?

PRAYER FOR THE DAY

Write a prayer of thanks to God for all He has shown you through this journey. Choose at least one of these truths, and thank Him for it. Ask Him to speak these truths over you as you walk with Him.

TRUTH, LIES, AND ACTION

Trading lies for truth has proven essential in this battle with shame. Standing on the truth is the only solid way out of hiding. With that said, here it is! Our last time for Truth, Lies, and Action:

TRUTH: A new way of looking at a truth from God's Word to replace the →
LIES: We want to name the lies we've believed and reclaim them with new truths to move us into →
ACTION: Because faith without works is dead (James 2:20), we want to be people of action. We will be looking today and tomorrow at specific action steps we can take to come out of hiding.

Our memory verse says:
"My son," the father said, "you are always with me, and everything I have is yours. But we had to celebrate and be glad, because this brother of yours was dead and is alive again; he was lost and is found." (Luke 15:31–32)

TRUTH: TRUTH tells us our Father will rejoice when we are made alive and are found. He will go to great lengths to find us when we are hiding and even running from Him. His pursuit never relents.

What other truths did you discover this week?

LIES: The LIE tells us many things. It tells us we are not worth being found. It tells us we are not worth pursuing. It tells us we may as well stay lost. These are all lies.

What other lies did you discover this week?

ACTION: Over the next few days, consider one of these action steps to help you take back the megaphone and come out of hiding:

- Find one trustworthy friend and share something you learned about yourself this week.
- Look back over your Action Steps over the last five weeks. Are there action steps you are still working on? If so, write them below and ask Jesus to give you the strength to move forward in them. Are there actions you took that changed things? Then write them below and celebrate with Jesus!

- As we close out the study, what are your new actions steps? How is God calling you to live from here on out? Write those below.

PRAYER OF THE DAY

Write a prayer of thanksgiving to God for the truths He has revealed through the pages of this study in your time with Him. Write a prayer asking Him to solidify truths that need to grow deeper roots. Ask Him to reveal how He has been working on your behalf through time in your story.

CONCLUSION

YOU HAVE A STORY TO TELL

From your first breath, God has been writing your story. Your story is filled with drama, intrigue, action, comedy, and tragedy. Through it all, God has been and is present. He holds every moment of your story—both the beautiful and the tragic. Nothing has been outside His view.

We live in a broken Eden, a failed paradise. The entrance of sin ushered the entrance of pain. Now every person has a shattered story. Pain is a part of living in a fallen Eden, and it doesn't discriminate. It touches us all.

Pain and shame keep us from telling our stories. We don't want to relive the hurt of the pain we've endured, so we stay silent. We're afraid of what others might think of what happened to us or what we have done, so we keep quiet. A wise woman once told me we should be good stewards of our pain. When you share the difficult parts of your story with people who are in the arena fighting with you, it changes the game. Your story has the power to heal others. Those who are recipients of the gift of your story find hope in the power of redemption. They begin to think about their own stories and the ways God has shown up in their past.

Your story matters more than you think. It matters to God because He authored it. He knows every detail and loves you anyway. It matters to those who need to hear it so they can heal. They need to know they are not alone. It matters in the story of the church, as well. Throughout the Old Testament, God commanded Israel to remember. He requested they build memorial stones so their children would ask about them and the story of what God had done could be told (Joshua 4:6–7). Telling our stories shows the power of God. It reminds those who have forgotten what God is capable of. It strengthens our faith. It grows our trust in God in places where we have lost it, both for those who need to hear it and for us as we tell it again. Every time I tell a part of my story, I'm reminded of God's ability to use what was meant to harm me and turn it into something remarkably good. I'm also astounded by the people who will say, "Me, too." There are always people who can relate and are reminded of God's faithfulness in their own lives.

> **Whenever you voice what God has done in your life—whether through the joy or the pain—you declare who He is.**

Our stories are still being written. We don't know what the rest of our stories hold, but we do know something about our future. Revelation 12:10 tells us what will happen to our enemy. We know the salvation and the power and the kingdom of our God and the authority of His Christ will come. We know the accuser of our brothers, the devil himself, the one who accuses before our God day and night, will be hurled down, defeated. In the end, the accuser loses, and our God wins. The war will come to an end, and we will be the victors!

In Revelation 12:11, we see how speaking our stories plays a role in defeating the enemy. "They triumphed over him by the blood of the Lamb and by the word of their testimony." Because of Jesus' blood *and* by speaking their stories, they overpowered the enemy. Whenever you voice what God has done in your life—whether through the joy or the pain—you declare who He is. You demonstrate with hard evidence what God is capable of doing. It's no wonder the enemy wants us to live in shame and stay quiet about our stories. If we speak, people will see God for who He really is—a Redeemer, a Healer, a Defender, a Rescuer, a Savior, and a King.

The devil is filled with fury because he knows his time is short (Revelation 12:12). He is motivated to fight against us. He will do his best to silence you with shame. He will wound you any way he can. But our God is greater and stronger and mightier.

Your story is woven into the fabric of the grand story of God—the tapestry God has been crafting since the beginning when shame didn't exist. When you hold tightly to your megaphone, turn it up, and share your story, you will hurl down the enemy and God will be glorified.

You are an overcomer, so don't stay silent.

Be bold.

Be courageous.

You are found.

You have a story to tell.

A WORD ABOUT STEWARDING YOUR STORY

Working through your story can be messy. My favorite resource for stewarding your story is the "My Life Story" map from *Listening to My Life*, a series of maps co-authored by Sharon Swing and Sibyl Towner. You can purchase a single map online at their store at www.onelifemaps.com.

As you are working through your story, find a counselor, a spiritual director, or a trusted friend who can walk with you. Uncovering painful memories can be difficult. Continuing to work through whatever you unearth with godly counsel is important. Remember, we share our broken stories with people who can bear the weight of them. Not everyone deserves to hear. Pray to God asking Him to reveal who can help you work through your story.

I pray you see the threads of God and of grace woven through your story right alongside the pain. I pray God reminds you of the joy you have had, as well. When you share your story, I pray it will be heard with compassion and it will not only change you, but all who hear it.

MY DEEPEST GRATITUDE—

To the "Tribe Crazy Train"—You girls are the real deal. Thank you for the amazing ways you surround each other and allow God to do His thing. You all are the answer to years of prayers for deep friendships. Your encouragement helped make this happen. Thank you for your courage to be real and to share your stories. You've made it possible for me and so many others to come out of hiding. I love you all.

To Sibyl—for teaching me to steward my story well and for creating a safe place to be vulnerable. You helped me find my voice.

To Judy—Your grace to a first-timer has been beautiful. You've made my first rodeo a grace-filled ride. You're a treasure. I am grateful to have a new partner in the kingdom who shares so many of my passions and who I can also call a friend. Thank you for believing in this message the way you have.

To My Church Family at The Creek—You have given me space to grow in Jesus and as a leader. I'm so grateful for the ways you have championed my gifts and equipped and empowered me. You've allowed me to fall down and extended the necessary grace to get back up again. I wouldn't want to be doing life anywhere else.

To Mom and Dad—For teaching me that Jesus loves me and always making me feel like I belong. You showed me that I am found from my beginning.

To Abigail—You have taught me so much in your short years of living. You show me how important and powerful grace is. You're going to do great things for the kingdom. I love you bigger than the world.

To Matt—For being my biggest fan and greatest partner in this crazy journey. Besides Jesus, you are the best part of my story. I'm so glad God chose to weave our stories together. I wouldn't want it any other way. I'm blessed to be yours.

To Jesus—For making a place for me at the table. Even in my mess, You made a way for me to belong. It cost You Your life, and You did it anyway. I owe You everything.

Discipleship Resources

978-0-8024-1382-6   978-0-8024-1343-7   978-0-8024-1340-6

Moody Publishers is committed to providing powerful, biblical, and life-changing discipleship resources for women. Our prayer is that these resources will cause a ripple effect of making disciples who make disciples who make disciples.

Also available as ebooks

MOODY
Radio™

*From the Word **to Life***

Moody Radio produces and delivers compelling programs filled with biblical insights and creative expressions of faith that help you take the next step in your relationship with Christ.

You can hear Moody Radio on 36 stations and more than 1,500 radio outlets across the U.S. and Canada. Or listen on your smartphone with the Moody Radio app!

www.moodyradio.org